George Washington

George Washington

Uniting a Nation

Don Higginbotham

A Madison House Book

ROWMAN & LITTLEFIELD PUBLISHERS, INC.
Lanham • Boulder • New York • Oxford

ROWMAN & LITTLEFIELD PUBLISHERS, INC.

Published in the United States of America
by Rowman & Littlefield Publishers, Inc.
A Member of the Rowman & Littlefield Publishing Group
4720 Boston Way, Lanham, Maryland 20706
www.rowmanlittlefield.com

12 Hid's Copse Road, Cumnor Hill, Oxford OX2 9JJ, England

British Library Cataloguing in Publication Information Available

Library of Congress Cataloging-in-Publication Data

Higginbotham, Don.
  George Washington : uniting a nation / Don Higginbotham.
     p. cm.
Includes bibliographical references and index.
  ISBN 0-7425-2208-3 (cloth : alk. paper)
  1. Washington, George, 1732-1799—Contributions in nationalism. 2.
Nationalism—United States—History—18th century. 3. National
characteristics, American. 4. United States—Politics and
government—1775-1783. 5. United States—Politics and
government—1783-1809. 6. Political culture—United
States—History—18th century 7. Presidents—United
States—Biography. I. Title.
  E312.17 .H636 2002
  973.4'1'092—dc21

                                                        2002005350

Printed in the United States of America

♾™ The paper used in this publication meets the minimum requirements of
American National Standard for Information Sciences—Permanence of Paper
for Printed Library Materials, ANSI/NISO Z39.48-1992.

To
Mary Claire
Chase
David Don
Stephanie

Contents

~

Acknowledgments

This small volume, initially a lecture, grew over a three-year period, most notably during the year 1999, the bicentennial of Washington's death. It did so because I had numerous opportunities to speak on Washington. On most occasions I returned to the original version of this book, "Washington the Unifier," because the subject continued to intrigue me. Of course, I did not inflict on my audiences a presentation of its current length. But even shorter versions saw the incorporation of new thinking on the subject. Since 1998 I have given lectures on aspects of this topic at the following: the Anderson House, headquarters of the Society of the Cincinnati in Washington, D.C., Columbia University, the New York Historical Society, and the Virginia Historical Society. Certain parts were given as talks at Monticello and Mount Vernon. Peter R. Henriques and Philander D. Chase read the penultimate draft and offered valuable suggestions on improving the contents, to say nothing of catching embarrassing errors. I continue to learn about Washington and his times from Stuart Leibiger and Robert McDonald, my former graduate students who are now established scholars in their own right. Brian Steele, now winding up his graduate career at the University of North Carolina, has assisted me in countless ways. Joseph E. Ellis was always ready to take time from his own superb scholarly work to respond to ideas about Washington and his "Founding Brothers." Jim Rees, the director at Mount Vernon, and his able staff at Washington's home have encouraged and assisted me over the years. I thank my friend John Kaminski of Madison House for his interest in my manuscript, which is greatly improved because of his labors. Rosalie Radcliffe, my secretary, continues to enable me to turn out an occasional manuscript, always with a keen eye to addressing my stylistic frailties, to say nothing of advancing my limited word-processing knowledge. Not all of my grandchildren are old enough to read this book, but I think they will nonetheless appreciate the dedication. Let me add that everything I accomplish owes much to the Higher Power in my life, my dearest wife Kathy.

~

Abbreviations

Frequently cited primary sources and biographies are referred to by the following abbreviations:

GW: Writings: John C. Fitzpatrick, ed., *The Writings of George Washington from the Original Manuscript Sources*, 39 vols. (Washington, D.C., 1931–1944)

GW Papers: W. W. Abbot et al., eds., *The Papers of George Washington*, in progress (Charlottesville, Va., 1983–), cited by series:

> *GW Papers: Col. Ser.: Colonial Series* (10 vols., completed)
> *GW Papers: Rev. War Ser.: Revolutionary Series* (12 of 40 vols. published to date)
> *GW Papers: Conf. Ser.: Confederation Series* (6 vols. completed)
> *GW Papers: Pres. Ser.: Presidential Series* (11 of 20 vols. published to date)
> *GW Papers: Ret. Ser.: Retirement Series* (4 vols. completed)
> *GW Papers: Diaries:* Donald Jackson and Dorothy Twohig, eds., *The Diaries of George Washington*, 6 vols. (Charlottesville, Va., 1976–1979)

Documentary History Ratification: Merrill Jensen, John P. Kaminski, Gaspare J. Saladino et al., eds., *The Documentary History of the Ratification of the Constitution*, 16 vols. to date (Madison, Wis., 1976–)

Freeman, *Washington*: Douglas Southall Freeman, *George Washington: A Biography*, 7 vols. (New York, 1948–1957)

Flexner, *Washington*: James Thomas Flexner, *George Washington*, 4 vols. (New York, 1965–1972)

CHAPTER ONE

❧

Unity and Symbolism

In delineating George Washington's most significant contributions to American nation-building in the last quarter of the eighteenth century, one finds perspective on that subject by looking at sixteenth-century Italy. Although the Italian Renaissance produced dazzling intellectual and artistic accomplishments, it generated no seminal idea or institution that would bind together its peoples. No Italian patriot experienced more pain from the fractious, conspiratorial character of politics in the city-states than Niccolo Machiavelli. In *The Prince* (1513), he voiced the hope that Italians, beginning with his own Florence, would one day act like their great Roman ancestors by showing political strength and patriotism before the powerful European states such as Spain and France, which feasted on the weaknesses of their divided Italian neighbors.

The American Revolution, in contrast, saw the emergence of both the idea of nationhood and the institution of a written constitution that would serve to unite, slowly but surely, the American people during the age of the American Revolution

1

and the Early Republic. George Washington, more than anyone else during the Revolutionary generation, both by word and deed, advanced the concept of an American nation and pressed for the creation of an institutional umbrella to bind America together. To these tasks, Washington brought a mindset, not a blueprint. He left the details of the latter to James Madison, James Wilson, Gouverneur Morris, Alexander Hamilton, John Dickinson, and others.

It is easy to exaggerate the ease with which George Washington and his fellow revolutionaries created a new polity on the western shore of the Atlantic. It might appear that the centrifugal winds at work in today's world had somehow always skirted America, except for the Civil War era. They now blow fiercely in what Pascal Boniface, a French scholar, calls "the secessionist age." The tendency is to dismantle large structures in favor of creating seemingly myriad small ones characterized by homogeneity of ethnicity and religion. Pluralism, whether geographic, cultural, or something else, seems unacceptable in much of the world. One need only look at what happened in the Soviet Union, Yugoslavia, and Czechoslovakia. Multiplicity even suffered from attack in parts of western Europe such as Spain, to say nothing of the tragedy of ethnic cleansing in the Balkans. Nor did it rank as an acceptable ideal in much of the Middle East and Africa or in India and Indonesia.[1]

The task of unity appeared daunting to the leaders of the American Revolution. Although there were, from a modern perspective at any rate, merely modest cultural differences between the white inhabitants of New England, the Middle Colonies, and the South, ethnic diversity had nevertheless increased markedly during the first six decades of the eighteenth century. And the phenomenal upsurge in the overall population during that period from a quarter of a million to two and a half million—a tenfold growth—had taxed provincial governments and local units of administration. Nothing brought regional fissures to the surface as quickly as the colonists' concerns about sharing the burdens of Britain's international wars, especially with reference to an intercolonial union within the British empire. Connecticut and Massachusetts hardly stood alone in maintaining that in Benjamin Franklin's proposed Plan of Union in 1754 New England would bear the brunt of the fiscal and military burden because the Southern provinces had never carried their share of the load during the imperial wars.[2] Suspicions and mistrust flared at any mention of intercolonial cooperation. The geographic regions also lacked internal solidarity. Most colonies quarreled with their neighbors over boundaries. New Yorkers and New Hampshirites fought over Vermont. Virginia and Pennsylvania set up overlapping counties in what eventually became southwestern Pennsylvania. Connecticut also challenged Pennsylvania's boundary claims. As a result, militia officers in the Wyoming Valley of northeastern Pennsylvania held commissions from Connecticut and refused to answer to Pennsylvania officials even after a Confederation commission ruled in 1783 that the valley rightfully belonged to Pennsylvania. Only through force did Pennsylvania subdue the rebellious Connecticut settlers. North Carolina and South Carolina contended with severe friction between their backcountry and coastal areas.[3] American loyalties in the mid-eighteenth century belonged first of all to their individual colonies or to the mother country, not to British-America in some collective sense.[4]

Franklin hardly spoke alone in voicing such views, but none exceeded him in reaching a broad audience in thrusting home the point. With the first steps toward an American national union only fifteen years away, he assured British readers in 1760 that American fragmentation promised to be a permanent condition. The crown's "fourteen separate governments on the maritime coast of the [North American] continent" were "not only under different governors, but have different forms of government, different laws, different interests, and some of them different religious persuasions and different manners." The provinces' differences were "so great that however necessary and desirable an union of the colonies has long been, for their common defence and security against their enemies, and how sensible soever each colony has been of that necessity, yet they have never been able to effect such an union among themselves, nor even to agree in requesting the mother country to establish it for them."[5] Andrew Burnaby, an English traveler, agreed with the veteran Pennsylvania printer and colonial agent. He asserted that "nothing can exceed the jealousy and emulation" that the provinces felt for one another. "Were they left to themselves, there would soon be a civil war from one end of the continent to the other." James Otis echoed that opinion in 1765: "America would be a mere shambles of blood and confusion without the mother country's guiding hand."[6] Both the radical Thomas Paine and the conservative John Dickinson voiced such fears during the War of Independence. This thinking, quite extensive in the circles of London officialdom, scarcely disappeared there after Yorktown and the Treaty of Paris in 1783. Sooner or later, it was said, Britain would have to pick up the pieces.

Yet history abounds with astounding surprises. People who have lived through the wholly unforeseen revolutions of 1989 in Eastern Europe and the subsequent dismemberment of the Soviet Union should be aware of the pitfalls of predicting future events, large and small.[7] Britain at this very period, in the years just after 1763, had reached a new level of unity and national feeling. If Linda Colley is correct, people often define themselves partly by what they are not; therefore, we can understand why the colonists defined themselves as *not* being Americans. They were British and they went to great pains to be seen that way because of what they did and what they acquired. What particularly attracted provincials on the western shores of the Atlantic world were manifestations of urban and gentry life, including the rise of consumerism, as practiced in England and to some degree in Scotland, Wales, and Anglo-Protestant Ireland.[8] As for the Britishness of the mother country, it grew from two developments that overlaid older, still existing eighteenth-century loyalties. As Linda Colley explains, a sense of a British nation, superimposed on old values and ties, stemmed from "a series of massive wars between 1689 and 1815 that allowed its diverse inhabitants to focus on what they had in common . . . and that forged an overseas empire from which all parts of Britain could secure real as well as psychic profits."[9] From the perspective of the colonists, they too shared in positive feelings about these British accomplishments, just as they saw themselves further linked to the mother country by still other things that they were not: Catholic and French. Indeed, anti-"Romanish" and anti-Gallic sentiments were deep-seated in both the British Isles and the New World dominions.

British unity existed alongside British colonial disunity. British unity spawned an imperious attitude toward the American colonies that led to parliamentary taxation of the peripheries and imperial reorganization in respects that were unprecedented and humiliating to colonists from New Hampshire to Georgia. A permanent American union—in fact, an independent American nation—would not have occurred in the eighteenth century had it not been spurred by a form of British national feeling that people in the metropolis were unwilling to share equally with Britons throughout the empire. "Rule Britannia," recently composed, meant not only to rule the seas and to stand unrivaled as the dominate "super power" in Europe but also to bring the weight of a patriotic nation down on distant settlements that seemed more concerned with going their own way than with showing proper deference and cooperation in responding to imperial laws and edicts.[10]

Colonial Americans resisted, blindly at times, seeing reality. In 1763, they endeavored to join the chorus of British nationalism and patriotism. After all, their Britishness, as they reckoned, was what they had in common with each other and with the mother country. It took them nearly a dozen years to face the truth completely: Britain had aggressively rejected their sense of kinship and the degree of autonomy that, in a *de facto* sense, they had long cherished in the imperial system. They had erroneously attributed their mistreatment mainly to a knot of ministers and to factional politics in Parliament.[11] Beginning perhaps as early as 1774, following the Intolerable Acts, British-Americans needed a new sense of community. It was not easy since they seemingly lacked building blocks, given their entrenched British-centeredness. There is substantial evidence that Englishmen, not the colonists, began the practice of speaking of the distant inhabitants of Virginia, Pennsylvania, and the other transoceanic dependencies as Americans and referring to those components of the empire as America.[12] Is it consequently any wonder that the need for unity became Washington's preoccupation, nay, obsession?—he who previously had been as addicted to British ways as any Virginia planter.[13]

And for those American elites who had felt deep insecurities because they failed to measure up, in British eyes, to standards of cultivation and gentility in metropolitan high society, they could counter by offering Washington as a model to emulate. If other Americans were like Washington in some important respects, and surely there must be many, then they could cast off what Franklin saw as a profound sense of comparative inadequacy and inferiority. Washington, the master of Mount Vernon, gave the lie to notions that all provincials lacked grace, refinement, and the finest amenities. Americans, as Washington's life portrayed, were a virtuous people, at odds with the claims of home country arbiters that parvenu colonial elites were crude materialists and often corrupt—ideas that "remained alive and well in English writing at the end of the colonial period."[14]

Washington stood out as a French and Indian War hero and a man of modesty, disinterestedness, and public spirit. Congressmen John Adams of Massachusetts and Silas Deane of Connecticut took heart from the presence of a Virginia leader of such martial accomplishments. Washington still looked quite young and vigorous, reported Deane, with "an easy Soldierlike Air, & gesture." Both New Englanders had heard the rapidly spreading story that Washington, before departing for the First Continental Congress in August 1774, had expressed, in elegant language, such concern for the beleaguered Bostonians that he had offered to raise a thousand men at his own expense and march them to the aid of Massachusetts. Although apparently untrue, the tale accurately portrayed Washington's rapid rise in the Virginia resistance movement. He chaired his Fairfax County's much-publicized, strongly-worded resolves. He staked out for himself an equally firm position at the subsequent Virgina Convention, which gave him the third highest number of votes of the seven delegates elected to the Congress, even garnering more than Patrick Henry.[15]

Here, in Washington, we have the beginnings, if no more than that, of an effort to find an American identity, but that was hardly a task completed in the short run, although the endeavor worked to Washington's advantage in public life as we shall see. Initially, the Virginian "validated the American gentry's own independent worth as an elite." Washington's appeal in 1775 to the Continental Congress and the colonial leadership in general was in part his personification of the British genteel ethos at its best. Furthermore, in his personal life and in his public commitment, Washington seemed to exemplify the life that Congress urged Americans to undertake: a self-imposed regime of self-denial and sacrifice.[16]

From the moment of his appointment as commander in chief of the Continental army to his retirement from the presidency over two decades later, Washington maintained his focus on American unity. He seems to have seen himself as an American from the moment of his appointment in 1775, if not before. Was it an epiphany of some sort? In any case, given the lack of direct evidence on the question, the historian has only speculation, not certainty, to employ. Speculation leads to the view that his extensive travels in the colonial West, his military service in the Seven Years' War with British and colonial forces, his journeys on the Atlantic seaboard as far north as Boston, and his deepening involvement in the resistance movement in the decade prior to Lexington and Concord gave him a high-ground or continental perspective on the thirteen colonies unknown to virtually every member of the Continental Congress. Of course, some congressmen had broadened their horizons by extensive travel; but the point to stress is that so many had not. It seems improbable that John and Samuel Adams, pillars of the patriot movement and influential in Congress, had ever traveled outside of Massachusetts before journeying to Philadelphia for the meetings of the delegates. Only Franklin, with years in Britain and with his detailed knowledge of America (he served as colonial agent at one time or another for seven of the North American provinces) could rival Washington's breadth.[17]

Washington's behavior also demonstrates that he sensed or knew, earlier and more fully than most of his countrymen, that various ingredients constitute the cement of nationhood. Some are symbolic in nature; and in the absence of long-shared national symbols on the part of a people whose previous imagery had come from British monarchy and kingship, Washington emerged as the most visible and meaningful sign of American cohesion throughout the independence struggle. He hardly needed the bibliographical trappings of a modern social scientist to realize that some measure of togetherness usually precedes political community, and Americans appeared almost wholly bereft of such symbolism at the outset of the struggle for independence, lacking as they did flags, anthems, great charters, and larger-than-life heroes ensconced in an American pantheon. Nor had they sought them in their dozen-year controversy with Britain, for they prefaced their arguments with profusions of their British-ness, including their contention that they were defending the liberties of Englishmen both at home in the realm and in the colonies. We have not been sufficiently mindful of the extent to which Washington recognized both his symbolic importance for his countrymen and his need to exploit that symbolism.

Thomas Jefferson in his oft-quoted assessment of Washington in 1814, though generally favorable to his fellow Virginian, criticized him for being preoccupied with ceremony and pageantry. During Washington's presidency, declared Jefferson, "I was ever persuaded" that he believed that America "must at length end in something like a British" constitutional monarchy. That belief "had some weight in his adoption of the ceremonies of levees, birthdays, pompous meeting with Congress, and other forms of the same character, [all] calculated to prepare us gradually for a change and to let it come on with as little shock as might be to the public mind."[18] It is a harsh judgment that fails to see Washington's presidential formalities in the context of how his countrymen had insisted on treating him from 1775 on: the endless dinners and receptions during the war and after wherever he appeared, the festivities that marked his arrival in Philadelphia for the Constitutional Convention, the observances that slowed to a snail's pace his journey to New York to be inaugurated as president, and the receptions held in his honor on his presidential trips throughout the nation during his first administration designed to take a reading on the condition of the union.

Surely Washington wished to capitalize on these ritualistic tributes, although not for material gain or personal authority. He deigned not to replace George III with George I, although Abigail Adams said he looked more like a reigning prince than the Hanoverian. So did Dr. Benjamin Rush: "there is not a king in

Europe that would not look like a valet de chambre by his side."[19] Tall and graceful in his body language, a man of few but well chosen words, he displayed a natural reserve that elicited respect, and, from some, even awe. "If he was not the greatest president," the dumpy, petulant John Adams grudgingly conceded, "he was the best actor of the presidency that we have ever had."[20] People who met him early in his Revolutionary military service gave strikingly similar descriptions. They spoke of his "dignity with ease and complacency," his "martial dignity," and "his gallant bearing and commanding figure."[21] Though a sensitive, proud human being, he remained a modest one. He employed his personal prestige and influence—manifestations of his role as a unifier—to promote American oneness: first to win the war and then to secure independence in a hostile world.

Because he ultimately succeeded in these roles, it seems appropriate to call him Washington the Unifier. The notion is particularly valid in view of his times, which in important respects still belonged to the Early Modern Era, the two hundred and fifty years or so before the Revolution. Leaders not uncommonly received designations that were affixed to their Christian names. Sometimes the appellations came from official bodies, as in the case of Peter the Great, and at other times from a wellspring of popular sentiment, as happened to Catherine the Great. Other examples come to mind: William the Silent of the Netherlands, who, though gregarious by nature, proved thoughtful and reflective when politics dictated otherwise; John the Steadfast of Saxony, who refused to be intimidated by Saxon's Catholics; and Frederick the Great, who himself became a unifier in ways not altogether different from Washington—his battlefield prowess against the odds of strong opposition kingdoms turned a poor and heterogeneous collection of territories into a formidable European power and in so doing became the fancy of his century. Even in America, where the colonists, seeing the connection between his victories and France's loss of Canada, named inns and taverns as well as ships "the King of Prussia." Catherine the Great added to the names of certain of her victorious generals their battlefield triumphs so those achievements could henceforth be a part of their personal and legal identities.[22]

These titles conferred on men what was perceived to be a kind of secular immortality. Though their republican proclivities would have made Revolutionary Americans stop short of such designations, we nonetheless see a kinship here between American and Early Modern European history. The leading lights of our Revolutionary generation likewise put a high premium on attaining the respect of their fellow citizens and, through them, of posterity. They would have heartily endorsed Voltaire's remark that the acts of great men deserve the attention of all time, serve as instruction to the young, and inspire devotion to the fatherland. Voltaire agreed with Rousseau's assertion in the *Social Contract* that the statesman "is the engineer who invents the machine."[23]

Voltaire and Rousseau hardly stand out as isolated exponents of such views. Enlightenment savants, declares Peter Gay, saw the highest legislator "as the embodiment of human energy, wisdom and rationality, as the founder of states, the preceptor of his country, the father of his people." These notions understandably resonated widely in Europe "before universal literary, before universal suffrage, before organized political parties, in an age when the political public was small."[24] Even in England with its parliamentary tradition, the political nation was tiny by later standards, and accordingly the monarch continued to play an essential role in public affairs. In the *Idea of a Patriot King*, Henry St. John, Lord Bolingbroke, urged Crown Prince Frederick, George II's heir, to eschew factions and special interests, restore an ancient morality, and reign in the interest of all the people. This kind of patriot ruler could be trusted with real powers because of his personal virtue and public-mindedness.[25]

Although Voltaire could argue that "almost nothing has ever been done in the world except by the genius and firmness of a single man,"[26] he nonetheless urged caution in formally recognizing the accomplishments of leaders: "for the great man is more difficult to be defined than the great artist. . . . It is more easy to name those to whom this high distinction should be refused than those to whom it should be granted." Oliver Cromwell ranked as a case in point. "All agreed that Cromwell was the most intrepid general, the most profound statesman, the man best qualified to conduct a party, a parliament, or an army, of his day." Yet "no writer ever gives him the title of great man" because he lacked virtue. The French philosopher saw another problem with honorifics: they might be bestowed prematurely.[27] It happened to France's own Louis XIV, who gained the title Louis the Great in 1680. On the other hand, Emperor Charles V, whose accomplishments outshone those of Louis XIV, failed to receive the title of great, and the sobriquet survived in Charlemagne merely as a proper name. Though excluding Cromwell from his list of exalted leaders, Voltaire did display a marked preference for soldier-statesmen; they were the subjects of his three biographies: Peter the Great of Russia, Louis the XIV of France, and Charles XII of Sweden. Since Voltaire died in 1778, he hardly lived long enough to make a comparison between Washington and Frederick the Great and Prince Eugene of Savoy, the last two respectively founders of the modern Prussian and Austrian states in the eighteenth century.[28]

These European comparisons indicate that some ingredients of emerging nationality in the Revolution were not distinctly American. In those older kingdoms, of course, individual statesmen symbolized unity, just as Washington did for an embryonic nation, whose people fought a long, arduous war of liberation. Still another interesting similarity is that republican Americans hailed Washington's virtue as his greatest quality. He impressed them, in words that appeared time and again with little variation, as "a great and good man." But it is doubtful if Americans praised the quality of virtue more than Bolingbroke and Voltaire, both of whom stated that virtue separated great leaders from average ones.[29]

Had Bolingbroke and Voltaire had an opportunity to leap forward in time and consult with Sigmund Freud, they might have agreed with the famous psychiatrist that the necessity of a father-image is so essential that men unfailingly endow someone with qualities of virtuous leadership whether or not such attributes exist.[30] Republicans though they were, countless Americans—or so their praise of Washington strongly indicates—were not averse themselves to some version of a great man theory of history. One of their literary favorites, David Hume, had himself spoken inconsistently on the matter. In *The Ideal of a Perfect Commonwealth*, an essay that stimulated James Madison's thoughts on factions and led him toward his position in the 10th Federalist on the feasibility of republics over vast geographic areas, Hume stood on its head Montesquieu's then-dominant small-republic thesis. Though an expansive republic might be harder to form than a small one, "there is more facility, when once it is formed, of preserving it steady and uniform, without tumult and faction." The principal danger, as Hume saw it, stemmed from the fact that the carving out of a vast territory "in a distant part of the world" might well require submitting to the control of a popular "single person," a warrior leader who subsequently might be engulfed by the flames of fame and "ends as an absolute monarch."[31] It was not inevitable, however, that the imposing leader, the symbol and force of unity in empire-building, do so. In *Of Parties in General*, Hume speculated that a modern statesman might someday reveal the wisdom and virtue of a Solon or a Lycurgus and fashion a new state in an expansive domain to promote the happiness and liberty of future generations. Hume died in 1776, unable to comprehend the on-going exertions of a Virginia planter in behalf of such an objective.[32]

There is an additional factor, biblical in nature, that may explain in part why the colonists focused on a single leader figure. We see in the voluminous sermon literature of the Revolutionary era analogies between the Hebrews, God's chosen people of old, and the colonists, his favored flock of a later day. Ministers reminded their congregations of the accomplishments of Moses against his Egyptian oppressors, and more than a few clergymen in New England and elsewhere exclaimed that Americans sought a deliverer from their own Egyptian bondage. Washington quickly emerged as the man. Both Washington and Moses, at about the same age, left the sweets of domestic life to take up the challenge against seemingly overwhelming odds. In March 1776, Washington himself heard a sermon by a Reverend Abiel Leonard celebrating the British departure from Boston. Drawing his text from Exodus xiv:25, the minister intoned that God "locked their chariot wheels, and caused them to drive heavily; and the Egyptians said, 'Let us flee from the face of Israel, for the Lord fighteth for them against the Egyptians.'" Even Washington's defeats could be minimized and seen as part of God's plan. His escapes became a sign of God's delivering the "American Moses" from his enemies so that he could fight another day.[33]

If Washington became a unifier, his symbolic role not wholly different from that of other leaders in Early Modern history, he also emerges as a transitional figure in terms of how Americans looked upon their statesmen. He was neither deified like a king whose authority ultimately came from God, nor did he receive the more modest forms of respect given to later American presidents, the kind encouraged by Jefferson, who detested ceremony and stressed simplicity in public and private activities during his own terms as chief executive. In truth, Washington fell somewhere in between—the only statesman in our history to receive plaudits of the kind that came from both the Old World and the New, that smacked both of monarchy and republicanism. (A favorite patriot cry was "God save great Washington.")

Washington served as the means by which Americans got monarchy out of their system without having to pay a fatal price for doing so, a rare instance of having one's cake and eating it too. For example, the linkage to kingship appears in the dedication of Revolutionary wartime performances of *Gustavus Vasa; or, The Deliverer of His Country*, a play about a Swedish monarch who repelled barbarian invaders. An epilogue written in 1782 implied eventual victory for America. The play, performed in postwar years on patriotic days, remained associated with Washington's name.[34] Artists employed European models because their national hero had to appear the equal of statesmen of the Old World, be it Washington the peerless general with the artillery piece at his side and horse at hand gazing on the field of honor or, after the Revolutionary War, as Cincinnatus, Pater Patriae. Consciously or not, some artists presented their work in ways that remind us of a reigning monarch or an antique hero.[35] Just as it had not been uncommon for colonial legislatures to commission statues or portraits of British royalty, so Congress in 1776 authorized a portrait of Washington to be painted by Charles Willson Peale, who a few years earlier had limned Washington at Mount Vernon. Peale's work—a native-born painter commemorating a native-born hero—honored Washington's expulsion of British General Sir William Howe's army from Boston. (On his personal initiative, John Hancock, the president of Congress, instructed Peale to also do a canvas of Martha Washington.) Peale's likeness of the general became the most important source for printmakers of the time.[36]

Whatever the nature of their praise of Washington, Americans engaged in various forms of appreciation for his talents and accomplishments. That only reaffirms Freud's caveat about the psychic needs of people collectively as well as individually. He became the idol of Massachusetts when his army forced Howe's evacuation of Boston. He received the acclaim of Harvard College, which gave him a Doctor of Letters, and of Massachusetts political dignitaries, who honored him with a dinner at the Bunch of Grapes Tavern.[37] Plays featuring Washington as the hero quickly followed, including John Leacock's *The Fall of British Tyranny* and a Boston play, attributed to Mercy Otis Warren, *The Motley Assembly*, in which a Captain Aid lifts a glass to the "godlike, glorious Washington."[38] As early as 1775 babies bore his name, which coincided with the appearance of the first book dedicated to him. In that first year of the Revolutionary War, the place names began to appear: Washington, North Carolina, and Washington Heights on Manhattan Island. As early as 1779, the public celebrated his birthday, the year of the first Washington biography, called a *Sketch of Mr. Washington's Life and Character*. John Bell, the author, asserted that "General Washington will be regarded by mankind as one of the greatest military ornaments of the present age, and that his name will command the veneration of the latest posterity."[39] Prints of Washington, often originating from the pens of unknown artists and reproduced by a variety of processes, began appearing soon after his appointment as commander in chief in broadsides, newspapers, and almanacs and in time appearing as mezzotints and on textiles such as kerchiefs. The general's image also showed up during the war on firebacks, buttons, buckles, ceramics, and glass. One broadside introduced the Virginian in music, entitled "Washington: A Favorite New Song in the American Camp."[40] A Pennsylvania German almanac in 1778 contains the first known reference to Washington as the Father of His Country ("Des Landes Vater"). Poets and essayists likewise hailed his character and accomplishments, ranging from the young slave woman, Phillis Wheatley, to Francis Hopkinson, who declaimed that "to him the title of Excellency is applied with peculiar propriety. He is the best and greatest man the world ever knew . . . neither depressed by disappointment and difficulties, nor elated with a temporary success. He retreats like a General, and attacks like a Hero. Had he lived in the days of idolatry, he had been worshipped as a God."[41]

Still other panegyrists, taking to the newspapers, asserted that he combined "the coolness of a Fabius, the intrepedity of an Hannibal, and the indefatigable ardour and military skill of a Caesar." As a statesmen too he had never known an equal since he shone "with unrivalled splendor in every department of life." "Brave without ostentation, magnificent without pomp, and accomplished without pride," he was "an honour to the human race, and the idol of America," a man "raised by Heaven to . . . guide the chariot of War."[42] Toasts to the tall Virginian, wishing him health and success, marked every fourth of July observance.

Whatever occasional doubts that surfaced about the commander in chief were few in number. Rumors in Congress and the army of a festering plot to remove Washington after his twin setbacks at Brandywine and Germantown in the fall of 1777 proved to be exaggerated. No evidence exists of an organized effort to supersede him with General Horatio Gates or anyone else. His slim knot of critics confined their expressed reservations to their personal correspondence. Nor was there much sympathy for the handful of men such as John Adams who believed that the adulation of Washington was unhealthy in a republican country. Yet any historical precedent belonged to Adams. Landon Carter, a Virginia planter who in 1776 knew Washington infinitely better than Adams did, voiced no alarms of a future Caesar at the head of the Continental army, although he could understand such fears from those who did not know his Old Dominion friend: "I never knew but one man who resolved not to forget the citizen in the soldier or ruler and that is G.W., and I am afraid I shall not know another." Had Carter lived to the end of the century and a bit beyond, he certainly would not have found another in Napoleon Bonaparte. The French emperor admitted he did not understand Washington's failure to grab power. Napoleon finally concluded that Washington, had he faced the internal and external problems of revolutionary France, would have been a fool not to seize the reigns of total authority. Under his own circumstances, explained Napoleon, "I could only be a crowned Washington."[43]

Notes

1. Pascal Boniface, "The Proliferation of States," *Washington Quarterly*, 21 (1998), 2–17.

2. *The Fitch Papers* (Connecticut Historical Society, Collections, vols. 17–18 [1918–1920]), 1:34–36; Albert B. Hart, *The Commonwealth History of Massachusetts . . .*, 5 vols. (New York, 1927–1930), 2:461.

3. Edmund S. Morgan, "Conflict and Consensus in the American Revolution," in *Essays on the American Revolution*, eds. Steven G. Kurtz and James H. Hutson (New York, 1973), 289–309; Peter S. Onuf, *The Origins of the Federal Republic: Jurisdictional Controversies in the United States, 1775–1878* (Philadelphia, 1983).

4. J. M. Bumsted, "'Things in the Womb of Time': Ideas of American Independence, 1633 to 1763," *William and Mary Quarterly*, 3d ser., 31 (1974), 533–64; Jack P. Greene, "The Seven Years' War and the American Revolution: The Causal Relation Reconsidered," *Journal of Imperial and Commonwealth History*, 8 (1980), 85–105.

5. Benjamin Franklin, *Interest of Great Britain Considered with Regard to her Colonies . . .* (London, 1760), in *The Papers of Benjamin Franklin*, eds. Leonard W. Labaree et al., 31 vols. to date (New Haven, Conn., 1959–), 9:90.

6. Andrew Burnaby, *Travels Through North America*, 3d ed. (1798; New York, 1904), 152–53; Edmund S. Morgan, *The Birth of the Republic, 1763–1789*, 3d ed. (Chicago, 1992), 6.

7. Paul Kennedy, in his much-acclaimed *The Rise and Fall of the Great Powers: Economic Change and Military Conflict from 1500–2000* (New York, 1987), suggested the possibility of overall decline for both the United States and the Soviet Union, with one or both losing its super power status at least in relative terms. He saw no reason to predict the collapse and dismemberment of the Soviet Union within a very short period of time.

8. Jack P. Greene has led the way in demonstrating the "mimetic impulses" of the colonists seeking to replicate British culture. See his *Pur-*

suits of Happiness: The Social Develoment of Early Modern British Colonies and the Formation of American Culture (Chapel Hill, N.C. and London, 1988) and his various other writings cited therein.

9. Linda Colley, "Britishness and Otherness: An Argument," Journal of British Studies, 29 (1992), 309–29, quotation on p. 316. To some extent, this article is a statement of themes fully developed in Colley, Britons: Forging the Nation, 1707–1837 (New Haven, Conn. and London, 1992). See also Kathleen Wilson, The Sense of the People: Politics, Culture, and Imperialism in England, 1715–1785 (Cambridge, England, 1995).

10. Jack P. Greene, "An Uneasy Connection: An Analysis of the Preconditions of the American Revolution," in Essays on the American Revolution, eds. Steven G. Kurtz and James H. Hutson (Chapel Hill, N.C., 1973), 32–80 and "The Seven Years' War and the American Revolution," 85–96. P. J. Marshall has also written extensively on British views on imperial centralization in the second half of the eighteenth century. For examples, see his "The British Empire in the Age of the American Revolution," in The American Revolution: Changing Perspectives, eds. William M. Fowler, Jr., and Wallace Coyle (Boston, 1979), 289–312 and "Empire and Authority in the Later Eighteenth Century," Journal of Imperial and Commonwealth History, 58 (1987), 105–23. Insightful too are various essays in Marshall, ed., The Oxford History of the British Empire, vol. 2: The Eighteenth Century (New York, 1998), esp. chaps. 1, 3, 5, 7, 10.

11. Greene, "Seven Years' War and the American Revolution," 97–105; Bernard Bailyn, The Ideological Origins of the American Revolution (Cambridge, Mass., 1967); T. H. Breen "Ideology and Nationalism on the Eve of the American Revolution: Revisions Once More in Need of Revising," Journal of American History, 84 (1997), 13–39. Bailyn and Breen, though viewing colonial ideology somewhat differently, both stress the deep anger and resentment, even the sense of betrayal, voiced by American protesters.

12. Breen makes the point and cites the literature to support it in "Ideology and Nationalism on the Eve of the Revolution," 30–31.

13. Don Higginbotham, "George Washington and Revolutionary Asceticsim: The Localist as Nationalist," in George Washington and the Virginia Backcountry, ed. Warren R. Hofstra (Madison, Wis., 1998),

223–50; Robert L. Dalzell, Jr., and Lee Baldwin Dalzell, *George Washington's Mount Vernon: At Home in Revolutionary America* (New York and Oxford, 1998), chaps. 1–3.

14. For these British perceptions and American reactions to them, see Michal J. Rozbicki, "The Curse of Provincialism: Negative Perceptions of Colonial American Plantation Gentry," *Journal of Southern History*, 53 (1997), 727–52 and *The Complete Colonial Gentleman: Cultural Legitimacy in Plantation America* (Charlottesville, Va., 1998), quotation on p. 101. See also Jack P. Greene, *Imperatives, Behaviors & Identities: Essays in Early American Cultural History* (Charlottesville, Va., 1992), chaps. 6, 7, 12. American attitudes about virtue are discussed in Charles Royster, *A Revolutionary People at War: The Continental Army and American Character, 1775–1783* (Chapel Hill, N.C., 1979), 17–25 and throughout; Greene, *Imperatives, Behaviors, & Identities*, chap. 9; and Ann Fairfax Withington, *Toward a More Perfect Union: Virtue and the Formation of American Republics* (New York, 1991).

15. John Adams Diary, [Aug. 29– Sept. 5, 1774] and Autobiography, Silas Deane to Elizabeth Deane, Paul H. Smith, ed., *Letters of Delegates to Congress*, 27 vols. (Washington, D.C., 1976–1998), 1:5, 12 n4, 61–62; "Fairfax Resolves," July 18, 1774, Washington to Bryan Fairfax, July 20, Aug. 24, 1774, W. W. Abbot et al., eds., *The Papers of George Washington: Colonial Series*, 10 vols. (Charlottesville, Va., 1983–1995), 10:119–28, 128–31, 155 (hereafter cited as *GW Papers: Col. Ser.*); Douglas Southall Freeman, *George Washington: A Biography*, 7 vols. (New York, 1948–1957), 3: illustration and note after 373. The following year, in balloting for Virginia delegates to the Second Continental Congress, Washington again obtained more votes than Henry. Freeman, *Washington*, 3:406.

16. Rozbicki, *Complete Colonial Gentleman*, quotation on p. 126. Withington, *Toward a More Perfect Union*, stresses Congress's campaign, beginning in 1774 in response to the Coercive Acts, to bring about a uniform moral code of behavior for Americans to strengthen their character and resolve in combating Britain.

17. Peter R. Henriques and Philander D. Chase, in reading an earlier draft of this essay independently of each other, both encouraged me to attempt an explanation of why and when Washington came to think of himself first and foremost as an American. That was assuredly the most

difficult question they put to me. John Shy offers ideas on these matters in his "Franklin, Washington, and a New Nation," American Philosophical Society, *Proceedings*, 131 (1987), 308–24. Shy argues that for both Franklin and Washington the process dated from 1774: "Their transition from imperial and provincial loyalties to national consciousness was not gradual but quite rapid." It is arguable that this was so, although the evidence is hardly overwhelming. But to speak of their "conversion to American nationalism" and to link it to their "extraordinary anger" for Britain appears extreme. Nationalism is a tricky word with distracting modern implications. Shy, quotations on pp. 318, 321.

18. Jefferson to Walter Jones, Jan. 2, 1814, Paul Leicester Ford, ed., *The Works of Thomas Jefferson*, 10 vols. (New York, 1892–1899), 9:446–51.

19. Benjamin Rush to Thomas Ruston, Oct. 29, 1775, in L. H. Butterfield, ed., *Letters of Benjamin Rush*, 2 vols. (Princeton, N.J., 1951), 1:91–94.

20. John A. Schutz and Douglas Adair, *The Spur of Fame: Dialogues of John Adams and Benjamin Rush, 1805–1813* (San Marino, Calif., 1966), 181.

21. These and other descriptions of Washington, with citations, appear in Catherine L. Albanese, *Sons of the Fathers: The Civil Religion of the American Revolution* (Philadelphia, 1976), 149.

22. Aleksei Orlov-Chesmenskii; Peter Rumiantsev-Zadunaiskii; Grigorii Potemkin-Tavricheskii.

23. Quoted in Peter Gay, *Voltaire's Politics: The Poet as Realist*, 2d ed. (New Haven and London, 1988), 180.

24. Quoted in Gay, *Voltaire's Politics*, 180, 181.

25. "The Patriot King," in *The Works of the Late Right Honorable Henry St. John, Lord Viscount Bolingbroke*, 5 vols. (London, 1754), 3:35–125.

26. Quoted in Gay, *Voltaire's Politics*, 181.

27. When the Russian Legislative Commission of 1767 wanted to designate Catherine II "The Great" and "Mother of the Fatherland," she declined, claiming that posterity alone could make such a judgment.

28. *The Works of Voltaire*, 42 vols. (New York, 1901), 9:319–24.

29. The best collection of contemporary American descriptions of Washington's qualities is John P. Kaminski and Jill Adair McCaughan,

eds., *A Great and Good Man:George Washington in the Eyes of His Contemporaries* (Madison, Wis., 1989). For a discussion of virtue in Voltaire's thinking, as well as the word's treatment in Diderot's *Encyclopedie*, see David Griffiths, "To Live Forever: Catherine II, Voltaire and the Pursuit of Immortality," in R. P. Bartless, A. G. Cross, and Karen Rasmussen, eds., *Russia and the World of the Eighteenth Century* (Columbus, Ohio, 1988), 446–68.

30. Sigmund Freud, *Leonardo da Vinci: A Study in Psychosexuality* (reprint; New York, 1947), chap. 6.

31. David Hume, *Essays, Moral, Political, and Literary*, 2 vols. (London [1875]), 1:480–81, 492.

32. David Hume, *Essays*, 127. Douglass Adair first pointed out Madison's debt to Hume in "'That Politics May Be Reduced to a Science': David Hume, James Madison, and the Tenth Federalist," in *Fame and the Founding Fathers: Essays by Douglass Adair*, ed. Trevor Colbourn (New York, 1974), 93–106.

33. Barry Schwartz, *George Washington: The Making of an American Symbol* (New York, 1987), 28–30; Robert P. Hay, "George Washington: American Moses," *American Quarterly*, 21 (1969), 780–91.

34. Jared Brown, *The Theater in America during the Revolution* (New York, 1995), 153–54.

35. Gary Wills, *Cincinnatus: George Washington & the Enlightenment* (New York, 1984).

36. Barbara Mitnick, ed., *George Washington: American Symbol* (New York, 1999), 57; Kenneth Silverman, *A Cultural History of the American Revolution* (New York, 1987).

37. Address from the Massachusetts General Court to Washington [c. March 28, 1776], W. W. Abbot, Philander D. Chase et al., eds. *The Papers of George Washington: Revolutionary War Series*, 12 vols. to date (Charlottesville, Va., 1985–), 3:555–57, 558–59 n1 (hereafter cited as *GW Papers: Rev. War Ser.*).

38. Dixon Wecter, *The Hero in America* (New York, 1941), 108.

39. Quoted in Mitnick, ed., *Washington American Symbol*, 68.

40. Wendy C. Wick, *George Washington an American Icon: The Eighteenth Century Graphic Portraits* (Washington, D.C., 1982), 77.

41. Mitnick, ed., *Washington American Symbol*, 106n; Francis Hopkinson, *Miscellaneous Essays*, 2 vols. (Philadelphia, 1792), 1:120.

42. The quotations, from American newspapers, are in Don Higginbotham, *The War of American Independence: Military Attitudes, Policies, and Practice, 1763–1789* (New York, 1971), 264. See also Kaminski and McCaughan, eds., *A Great and Good Man*.

43. Bernard Knollenberg, *Washington and the Revolution* (New York, 1940; Kenneth R. Rossman, *Thomas Mifflin and the Politics of the American Revolution* (Chapel Hill, N.C., 1952), chap. 11; Higginbotham, *War of American Independence*, chap. 9; Jack P. Greene, ed., *The Diary of Colonel Landon Carter of Sabine Hall, 1752–1778*, 2 vols. (Charlottesville, Va., 1965), 2:1042–43. Napoleon quoted in Susan Dunn, *Sister Revolutions: French Lightning, American Light* (New York, 1999), 129. Paul K. Longmore's insightful and stimulating *The Invention of George Washington* (Berkeley and Los Angeles, 1988), chaps. 14–17, is also interested in the major themes that I address in this book. Longmore's book is especially relevant to my first two chapters since his volume ends soon after the Americans declared independence.

CHAPTER TWO

~

Political Unity
and Consolidation

A shift in focus enables us to see how Washington used this reservoir of good will and symbolism to promote political unity, for that dimension of his public career gives the greatest meaning to the name Washington the Unifier. Had he demonstrated a respect for compromise and conciliation, displaying talents for bringing men together rather than driving them apart, in his life before the Revolution? Yes, in time he had, but the process hardly took place overnight, being noticeably absent during his first military career in the French and Indian War. Division rather than consensus prevailed in the Old Dominion. Some Virginians saw the conflict as provoked by their own province, designed to enrich western land speculators, including George Washington. Any Gallic threat seemed far away, impacting at most their remotest frontier areas. Tensions also flamed between the colony's militiamen and the better-trained officers and men of Washington's Virginia Regiment, a force that might be termed semi-professional. Washington himself provoked controversy. His relationship with Governor Robert Dinwiddie grew tense as he blamed the executive for problems not of his

making in providing supplies for the soldiers. The legislature—
"Chimney Corner Politicians"—also drew his ire for alleged tardiness in making appropriations. He refused to spare his military superior in 1758, British General John Forbes, an excellent officer, with whom Washington quarreled over the proper route to take against the French at Fort Duquesne, situated at the forks of the Ohio. Washington's real enemy turned out to be the neighboring colony of Pennsylvania, for he claimed that its dignitaries had hoodwinked Forbes into building a road westward through their province, a road that, in Washington's opinion, would later help Pennsylvania prevail over Virginia in the Ohio Valley trade.

How then did Washington progress from a chronic complainer to a unifier? Although he certainly remembered the discord of the French and Indian War, we cannot be sure he ever faced up to his own part in it. We can say with confidence that his seventeen-year career in the Virginia House of Burgesses, from 1758 to 1775, provides concrete evidence for the beginning of a different attitude. That body prided itself on harmony and consensus as much or more than any American legislature before the Revolution. If an occasional member of the House of Burgesses displayed maverick tendencies—Patrick Henry, for example—Washington did not. Washington behaved as a team player, including the years of growing crisis after 1763 between Britain and her New World dominions. He wished to take a stronger stand than most of his colleagues over the Townshend taxes, but he bowed to the majority. In 1774, in response to the Intolerable Acts, he accepted the fact that most burgesses showed more reluctance than he to go beyond non-importation of British goods and to refuse to export Virginia's agricultural products to the mother country, the latter being a much greater economic sacrifice.

By 1774 Washington also began to think of unity in intercolonial terms. He favored standing firmly with Massachusetts, even though Parliament aimed the Coercive Acts at the Bay colony.

Fortunately for Washington, most of his fellow Virginia legislators agreed with him that an intercolonial congress should meet, with the authority to coordinate resistance to Britain, including a systematic boycott of British goods. Subsequently, Virginia elected Washington a member of its delegation to the First Continental Congress in 1774 and to the Second Continental Congress the following year. Both Congresses displayed a striking degree of agreement in their methods of responding to Britain, even to taking control of the New England forces surrounding the British troops in Boston after the battles of Lexington and Concord. Washington had already revealed his readiness to take up arms in the common cause by wearing his Virginia military uniform as he sat in the Second Congress. His selection by Congress to command the New England army meant that it became a congressional army—or, as it was now called, a Continental army. He recognized that the appointment of a Virginian to command what still remained at that point a New England force served as a sign of the need for the unity of North and South in the common cause. Not surprisingly, the commander in chief eschewed congressional politics—he stayed aloof from factionalism within that body and he played no favorites, confining most of his communications to proper channels, which usually meant dealing with the president of Congress. John Adams in November 1775, six months into the war, declared that "in such a Period as this, . . . when Thirteen Colonies unacquainted in a great Measure, with each other, are rushing together into one Mass," only "a Miracle" would keep "Such heterogeneous Ingredients" from "violent Fermentations."[1]

During the year following Washington's appointment, the unity factor took on a new dimension. Should the colonists move from standing together in fighting for their British rights to supporting mutually a complete break with the mother country? Part of the problem at hand, said Adams, was could the extralegal Congress transform itself into something permanent—that is, could it successfully craft a continental union? Such an effort would be "the most intricate, the most important, the most dangerous, and delicate Business of all."[2] Washington favored separation from the empire as early as January 31, 1776, after reading Thomas Paine's harsh, inflammatory pamphlet *Common Sense*. Unwilling to embarrass Congress, he eschewed sharing those views with that body, although he implied them in an occasional private letter. Yet even more pain and suffering might be needed to push Congress over the edge. At the end of May, he voiced his frustrations with those congressmen who continued to hope that Britain would offer acceptable terms to terminate the imperial civil war. Still, he recognized that the intercolonial tribunal in Philadelphia must speak with one voice, whatever it did. For "if the House is divided, the fabrick must fall." Only "disunion can hurt our cause"; "prudence, temper, and Moderation . . . in our Council" must prevail.[3]

When John Hancock, the president of Congress, forwarded him a copy of the Declaration of Independence, Washington replied that the step had been necessary since no recourse remained under the crown. Washington informed his officers to assemble their brigades for a reading of the document that proclaimed a new nation: "The General hopes this important Event will serve as a fresh incentive to every officer, and soldier, to act with Fidelity and Courage, as knowing that now the peace and safety of his Country depends . . . solely on the success of our arms: And that he is now in the service of a State, possessed of sufficient power to reward his merit, and advance him to the highest Honors of a free Country." He capitalized the words "Country" and "State," a significant indication that he already thought of America as a nation in a firmer or more consolidated sense than most of his countrymen at the time.[4]

Just as he could not have played the political role without the previously mentioned symbolic role, so too his political influence would have been inconsequential had he not possessed some of the personal qualities so effusively assigned to him, and had he not compiled a solid record of performance as commander of the Continental army. Although his generalship was not marked by brilliant strategy and tactics, he displayed tenacity, persistence, and the power to command respect and admiration. Some years ago in a small book entitled *George Washington and the American Military Tradition* I sought to explain some of the other factors that accounted for his success as commander in chief, especially his efforts to build a well-trained professional army, his respect for civilian control, and his mediating role in disputes between Congress and the army.[5]

It became apparent from the moment of his appointment that political unity for Washington meant something twofold: creating a common bond in the army and bolstering the prestige and power of the Continental Congress, the central authority over the states. As early as July 4, 1775, in his general orders issued just two days after he arrived outside Cambridge to head the New England forces besieging Boston, the new commander in chief addressed both goals. Here, as Fred Anderson says, appears "the germ of a truly revolutionary idea" at that very early date: "American nationhood." "The Continental Congress," began Washington, "having now taken all the Troops of the several Colonies, which have been raised, or which may be hereafter raised, for the support and defence of the Liberties of America, into their Pay and Service, They are now the Troops of the United Provinces of North America; and it is hoped that all Distinctions of Colonies will be laid aside, so that one and the same Spirit may animate the whole, and the only Contest be, who shall render, on this great and trying occasion, the most essential service to the great and common cause in which we are all engaged."[6]

Laying distinctions aside meant hard work, even for Washington. Although he had warmly backed Massachusetts after the passage of the Coercive Acts and had sought agreement of sentiment and action as a member of Congress, he himself had to wrestle with conflicted feelings toward the New Englanders who constituted his army in the opening months of the conflict. Based on his own military experiences in the French and Indian War, Washington thought in terms of an army not unlike the British army he had served with in the 1750s, the army in which his half-brother at one time held an officer's rank, and the one in which he himself had sought a colonel's commission and British regular army status for his Virginia Regiment. New Englanders, on the other hand, influenced by their own military backgrounds and their Puritan culture and religion, expressed aversion to the order, discipline, and lengthy service that Washington advocated. He knew that only such a force could stand up to Britain and be a nationalizing presence for Americans. He privately criticized the New England soldiers, although he admitted that the rank and file had potential as fighting men if better officers commanded them. The Massachusetts Revolutionary government also frustrated Washington by insisting on paying its Continental troops by the lunar month rather than by the calendar month, which gave them a monetary advantage. The commander in chief informed local leaders that Congress had instructed otherwise. The Bay colony practice, declared Washington, would "throw the rest of this Army into disorder." He warned James Otis, Sr., that if Massachusetts ignored Congress's intention, it would give "a fatal stab to the Peace of this Army . . . Lord North himself could not have devised a more effectual blow to the Recruiting Service." In time, Washington prevailed in all these matters—with a mixture of tact, diplomacy, and firmness—without losing the support of provincial chieftains. On Washington's leaving Massachusetts after the British army sailed away from Boston in March 1776, the colonial legislature praised him for respecting the rights and liberties of the citizens and respecting their civil institutions.[7]

If confronting New England's Puritan ways posed Washington's first challenge in dealing with his army, it marked only the beginning, for elsewhere he encountered less homogeneity than in Massachusetts and its regional neighbors. He spent the great majority of his war years in the middle colony-states, where heterogeneity characterized the population. New Englanders in the army had their problems with men from below the Hudson, and those soldiers from New York to Delaware fought and bickered with the Yankees and they did so among themselves as well. Time and again Washington urged the officers and men of the army to eschew religious, ethnic, and provincial jealousies. Some examples indicate the range of Washington's difficulties.

Tension over religion sometimes posed a threat within the army as well as between elements of the soldiery and the civilian population. Rivalries appeared between competing Protestant sects along with a general dislike of Catholics and Jews. Washington's first religious pronouncements to gain attention during the Revolutionary War appeared in the fall of 1775 in his instructions to Colonel Benedict Arnold prior to the invasion of Quebec, with its overwhelmingly Catholic population. Washington ordered Arnold to "restrain every Officer & Soldier" from infringing on "the free Exercise of the Religion of the Country" and "the Rights of Conscience in religious Matters with your utmost Influence & Authority."[8] Principal and policy explain Washington's attitude, just as both lay behind his banning of the annual celebration of Pope's Day in November 1775, highlighted by parades, banners, strong drink, and other, often riotous, activity, a practice particularly embraced by troops from Puritan New England. "There are no records of its celebration in America after 1775," declared Paul Boller, who gave Washington substantial credit, although a desire to influence French Canadians and to win the support of the French government played its part. Washington dealt another blow to religious prejudice when he upheld a Rhode Island regiment's choice of John Murray, father of American Universalism, for a chaplain's post in the army over the protest of orthodox chaplains, who condemned Murray's creed of salvation for all as heresy.[9] As Washington told Congress, any "tendency to introduce religious disputes into the Army . . . should be avoided," and therefore he favored each regiment's having the right to choose its own chaplain.[10]

Other challenges, seemingly more intractable, occupied Washington's time. Frontier riflemen from Virginia and Pennsylvania fought with Marblehead fishermen from Massachusetts. New England men did not want to serve under a New Yorker, General Philip Schuyler, and New Yorkers expressed similar attitudes about General Horatio Gates, a darling of the New Englanders. Washington's effort at the end of 1775 to make the army truly intercolonial and American by forming regiments consisting of men from more than a single colony met with total failure, although it did show his commitment to unification.[11] The army seemed to be a seething mix of men—and some women—of different races, nationalities, and socioeconomic backgrounds; of short-term and long-term enlistees, and of militia and regulars, the latter invariably condescending toward the irregulars. The numbers under Washington's immediate command fluctuated wildly, although in what became predictable ways, usually down to a few thousand in the winter and sometimes up to 15,000 or more in the warm weather months. Consequently, Continental regiments increased and contracted in number, their composition resembling a revolving door. Such units lacked the degree of institutional identity that existed in the British army of that day or of Union and Confederate regiments in the Civil War. Perhaps a low point in terms of regimental stability occurred at Valley Forge when Washington complained that "a Regt is scarcely the same a Week together."[12] At times it even proved difficult to determine who constituted the army, since, as Holly Mayer has demonstrated, many kinds of civilians, "men as well as women, black and white," formed an unofficial part of the service. Functions that later became militarized, such as nursing, remained privatized in the eighteenth century. Sutlers, teamsters, myriad artisanal types, laborers, wives, and other women, some though not all prostitutes, accompanied the army throughout the struggle.[13]

Yet Washington persevered, not only against his British adversaries but in holding his own army together.

An examination of Washington's general orders to the Continental army, issued over a period of eight and a half years, shows how repeatedly he preached the gospel of placing the unity of the army above sensitivities of every kind, including rank, pay, and retirement benefits. He bent over backwards to avoid favoritism to Virginia officers such as Colonel Daniel Morgan, whose record warranted a promotion sooner than he received it. At every disruption, he reminded his comrades in arms of their commitment to "the cause of our Common Country."[14] Some of the Continentals, especially officers, accepted Washington's gospel that they should think of themselves not as simply New Hampshirites, New Yorkers, and Virginians but as Americans as well. Washington enjoyed particular success in instilling esprit and national identity in younger officers—some of them at the senior level such as Nathanael Greene, Henry Knox, and Anthony Wayne; others at the field-grade level or company level, such as Alexander Hamilton, John Laurens, David Humphreys, Henry Lee, and John Marshall. Because of his wartime experiences at Germantown, Valley Forge, and Stony Point, recalled Marshall, "I was confirmed in the habit of considering America as my country and Congress as my government. I had imbibed these sentiments so thoroughly that they constituted a part of my being." He never made a secret of the fact that Washington was his idol, that his litmus test for anyone or anything was what Washington believed.[15]

If literacy rates for Revolutionary enlisted men failed to approach the level of troops in the Civil War, when it seemed as though almost every Billy Yank and Johnny Reb kept a diary or journal in his knapsack, we have enough evidence to say that Washington profoundly impacted the rank and file. From the vast collection of pension memoirs filed long after the Revolution, we find that countless memorialists recorded their impressions of Washington up close, recalling contacts with him and his personal acts. A scholar who has examined all the surviving pension applications writes: "Instead of the stiff, cold, aloof figure of Stuart portraits . . . Washington was, to his common soldiers, a warm, fatherly figure. In the dozens of pensions narratives that describe personal encounters with the general, he comes off in every instance as an approachable, athletic younger man. Literally thousands of men, especially in the dark winter of 1776 and 1777, when he made personal appeals for units to remain beyond their discharges, saw their service as a personal favor to their friend General Washington."[16]

Although officers' resignations, enlisted men's desertions, and jealousies between officers of different state lines and between regiments from different states hardly disappeared, Washington held his army together, despite humiliating defeats in New York and Pennsylvania in 1776 and 1777, and despite excruciating privations during virtually every winter of the war. As a person, he emerged as the most visible symbol of unity for Americans. And as an institution, his army stood out as the most visible symbol of unity for his countrymen. In his farewell message to the army in November 1783, he marveled "that Men . . . from the different parts of the Continent, strongly disposed . . . to despise and quarrel with each other," had become "one patriotic band of brothers."[17]

Of course, Washington's statement contained exaggeration, but that hardly mattered. He had expanded many minds, urging subordinates to focus on their accomplishments, which had been remarkable, and to build on those achievements for the benefit of the nation in the years ahead. But a growing degree of commonality and togetherness had come at what could have been a dangerous price. In *A Revolutionary People at War*, Charles Royster argues that the officers increasingly saw themselves as separate from an American society preoccupied with its own self-preservation and material gain at the expense of the army and its efforts at nationhood. That dangerous trend, which Washington deflated in his response to the disgruntled officers' Newburgh Addresses in 1783, showed that independence had both military and political dimensions.[18]

Over two decades and more Washington steadfastly promoted American unity under a central political system, be it under the extralegal Continental Congress during the war, under the Articles of Confederation in the 1780s, or under the Federal Constitution during his presidency. He wasted no time after assuming his military command in 1775. No rules or guidelines existed concerning the jurisdictional boundaries between Congress and the Revolutionary governments in the colonies. It may be little exaggeration to say that the concept of congressional primacy, to the extent that the colonies (and later states) acknowledge such superintendency from Philadelphia, first received explicit attention from Washington, who recognized that Congress alone should direct the army, for he should have only one civil superior.

His months with the army in New England stand out as the most significant of the war for relations between Congress and its army on the one hand and the soon-to-be independent states on the other. When New England leaders barraged him with requests for military aid hither and yon, he replied that they should instead contact the Philadelphia lawmakers. Since he held his commission from Congress, he took no orders from any colony or state government. (His concern for establishing precedents became evident once again during his presidency.)[19]

The states posed other delicate problems. Had Washington ridden roughshod over their jurisdictions, the thirteen former colonies would never have agreed to a firmer union in the following decade.

Though in the midst of a revolution, he respected state-level law and order to a remarkable degree. His resolve included turning over both enlisted men and officers accused of crimes to civilian courts. However understandable the patriotic "zeal" of his soldiers in pulling down and beheading the statue of George III at the south end of Broadway in New York City after the reading of the Declaration of Independence, Washington gently but firmly informed them that the destruction of property constituted unacceptable behavior, that "proper authority" in the city should have been given the opportunity to decide what to do with the equestrian symbol of a monarchy now rejected.[20]

His efforts to win the good will of local officials produced only limited benefits during the war, for the superstructures of the states were deficient. Governors had little authority to take quick, decisive steps, and constituent pressures intimidated legislatures from voting the taxes, supplies, and manpower required to gain independence. Though Washington acknowledged the difficulty of forging new political instruments in the midst of violent revolution, he felt disappointed that the very threat to the existence of America had not driven his countrymen to a greater show of unity. As he said countless times, the war revealed two glaring deficiencies in the political system of the United States: "the inability of Congress and the tardiness of the States" in meeting their responsibilities. "If we would pursue a right system of policy," he contended, then "we should all be considered, Congress, Army, &c. as one people, embarked in one Cause, in one interest; acting on the same principle and to the same End."[21]

Though never an original thinker, nor given to theoretical constructs, Washington favored adopting a different political system more consonant with the spirit of the nation and more capable of energy in public measures. Two major items headed his agenda. First, Congress must have the power to follow through on whatever broad responsibilities it had been delegated. Second, independent federal finances, by whatever means, were indispensable since no reform could be meaningful without the "powerful succor of money." Washington hated dependence. He said as much in fighting for his economic freedom from low tobacco prices and British creditors in the 1760s. He spoke now in the 1780s as an independent man who had fought for an independent nation, and who, as the prospect of military victory increased, now stepped up his fight for an independent Congress.

In response to a request from Congress, Washington penned the first of the three great state papers issued during his years in public life, all of which dealt with national consolidation. The first two documents resemble the third, his Farewell Address, which he presented to his countrymen near the end of his presidency. The earlier ones also reflect on the future needs of the country, coming as he prepared to resign his commission and as he awaited the news of the treaty of peace in Europe in 1783. Entitled "Sentiments on a Peace Establishment," the first called for a permanent postwar army at a time when many Americans believed that standing forces were a threat to liberty in time of peace. But Washington's plan advocated only an army modest in size, which he considered consistent with American concerns about a bloated military arm. More innovative, even daring, he urged a complementary line of defense in a uniformly trained and organized militia drawn from the states, a body set apart from the great bulk of the state militias. Here, in one of the few times he dealt in detail with the subject of a more cohesive centralized government, he spoke for putting under congressional jurisdiction a component of state power dearest to advocates of localism and states' rights.[22]

Skeptical that Congress could initiate reform, and in fact it never adopted his "Sentiments," Washington, in the second state paper, appealed to the states in June of 1783 in his so-called Circular Letter to look broadly at the condition of the union. Congress had twice proposed constitutional amendments to give the Confederation a modest independent revenue only to see the first one shot down by the states in the ratifying process, and the second one was encountering the same difficulties and would eventually fail as well. So, ironically and paradoxically, the states, the culprits, were the only hope. In the Circular Letter, Washington summed up arguments he had made throughout the war. First and foremost, the union must be preserved and Confederation must be invigorated so that the central government could meet the nation's needs. Only "one Federal head" could guarantee "an indissoluble Union." Reform could become a reality if Americans displayed a recognition of common interests and a determination to dispense with "local prejudices." His message carried implications for external relations as well: "It is only in our united Character as an Empire, that our independence is acknowledged, that our power can be regarded, or our Credit supported among Foreign Nations."[23]

Washington's failure to arouse the states to action hardly surprised him. Something of a pessimist, though given to occasional moments of optimism, he had feared that the coming of peace would erode the already fragile links of nationhood now that Britain was no longer an imminent threat. The government of the Confederation, which he had always considered inadequate, became even weaker as the states flouted its authority both in domestic and foreign affairs. Tensions and conflicts within the states during the mid-1780s—most notably Shays's Rebellion in Massachusetts—also threatened the stability of the country. Washington, thoroughly alarmed, feared the presence of "combustibles in every State."[24]

Was America disintegrating, going the way of the warring Greek city states? As Washington had said before, as he now said to Secretary at War Henry Knox, and as he would say later as well, the British had predicted these very developments resulting from independence.[25] Joseph Priestley, a staunch English friend of America, recalled that "it was taken for granted" in the parent kingdom "that the moment America had thrown off the yoke of

Great Britain, the different states would go to war among themselves." Washington and other Americans became increasingly fearful. "If we are afraid to trust one another," complained Washington, "there is an end of the Union."[26] Franklin reported a widespread belief that "our States are on the point of separation, only to meet hereafter for the purpose of cutting one another's throats."[27] John Murrin suggests that during the American Civil War "the Confederate sense of national identity appears to have been deeper, more profound, more passionate (no doubt more of a nationalism) than the ties that bound the Thirteen Colonies together from 1775 to 1783 and beyond."[28]

Between 1784 and the opening months of 1787 Washington, in retirement on the banks of the Potomac, seemed consumed with completing the last phase of his final reconstruction of Mount Vernon and reviving his domestic enterprises; but the problems of the Confederation government hardly escaped his concern. In fact, Mount Vernon became a kind of clearinghouse for advocates of shoring up the union. Letters came and went on the subject. It also produced lively discussions with Washington's unending procession of visitors to his estate. Along with the hordes of uninvited guests, he conversed on public issues with Virginians James Madison, Richard Henry Lee, and James Monroe and Generals John Cadwalader and the Marquis de Lafayette. Washington, in a sense, started the ball rolling for greater federal power when in 1785 he offered to host a conference of representatives from Maryland and Virginia. The conferees resolved jurisdictional and navigational matters over shared waterways, especially the Potomac River. The results led to more ambitious conclaves during the next two years to which all the states were invited.

By 1787, on the eve of the Constitutional Convention, Washington believed more fervently than ever that, as Alexander Hamilton phrased it in the concluding *Federalist* essay, "a nation without a national government is . . . an awful spectacle."[29] As early as 1783 he had voiced support for "a Convention of the People" as a way of altering the American political fabric. In 1786, he correctly predicted that the Annapolis gathering of state commissioners to deal with common commercial problems of the Confederation would fail. He thought its focus too narrow and the momentum for reform had hardly peaked. Early the following year he responded positively to letters from Henry Knox, John Jay, and James Madison, all seeking Washington's backing of a new system of political engineering that would restore the traditional three branches of government and clip the wings of state power as well. His enthusiasm stimulated these and other nationalists to try something bolder and more comprehensive than ever before attempted. As he told Henry Lee, his views about "Foederal Government" had long been "very well known" and "publickly & privately, have been communicated without reserve."[30]

Washington's name stood out as the foremost weapon of the nationalists on the eve of the delegates gathering at Philadelphia. The New York City press reprinted biographical sketches of America's most revered hero of the Revolution. The June 1783 Circular Letter, widely respected and reproduced at the time, was not forgotten. It again appeared before the readers of the gazettes, part of what has been described as "an avalanche of newspaper items" linking Washington to the concept of a stronger central political system. The Providence *United States Chronicle* predicted that America's fortunes would have been infinitely better had Washington's recommendation been adopted a few years earlier. The Philadelphia *Independent Gazetteer* hoped a re-reading of the letter might inspire its subscribers to aid in extricating the country from its "political degeneracy."[31]

Washington would not have made the trip to Philadelphia had he not been convinced that Madison and other influential men of like minds would strive tenaciously for the national goals he espoused.[32] Washington the Unifier had stressed his unwillingness to be a part of any half-hearted endeavor like the Annapolis Convention or any other undertaking that would undercut his standing as an apostle of national cohesion. Better to stay at home and make the fight with his reputation in tact at a more propitious moment than to be a part of another feeble effort to invigorate the nation.[33] Given those "well known" views, Washington's attendance at the Constitutional Convention and his willingness to serve as its president helped to thrust the delegates in the direction of a much more consolidated political system. Within his state's delegation, he gave firm support to Madison's Virginia Plan; it set the agenda from which the convention scarcely deviated. The plan in a general way contained ideas for greater political solidarity that Washington had voiced for years. And, in outline at least, he had expressed them to Madison before the convention, especially his conviction that the national government should have real power and that it should have the mechanisms for enforcing its laws. The details of the new instrument concerned him far less than the end product. He had said repeatedly that it must enable the government to create a sound military establishment, to generate revenues, to address the public debt, to promote foreign and domestic trade and commerce, and to further western development.[34]

Washington had argued that it was better to risk major changes in the national political structure rather than see the convention provide only feeble alterations for fear that the states would reject a vigorous new constitutional formulation. Though compromises had been necessary at Philadelphia, they had preserved much of the radical shifting of power from the states to the central government contained in the Virginia Plan. But he still questioned whether the public had suffered severely enough under the Confederation to accept such an astringent remedy.[35]

The Constitutional Convention launched the contest for ratification by associating the new instrument with Washington. The delegates might have forwarded their handiwork to the

Confederation Congress and to the public at large without significant comment; but they had a better plan in mind: "to prepare an Address to the people, to accompany the present Constitution, and to be laid with the same before the U—States in Congress." Drafted by Gouverneur Morris, member of the Convention's committee of style and signed by Washington, the president of the Convention put himself four-square behind the Constitution. Although he acknowledged that it would not meet with the complete approval of every state, he wanted it known that the Convention had been mindful of the states and the rights of the citizens. The document stemmed from "a Spirit of Amity" and "Deference & Concession" that pervaded the assemblage. Experience with the Articles of Confederation had demonstrated that the powers necessary for effective government could not be "fully and effectually vested" in "one Body of Men," a unicameral legislature. "Hence results the Necessity of a different Organization." He concluded by expressing the "hope" and conviction "That it may promote the lasting Welfare" of America, "a Country so dear to us all."[36]

It might be hard to exaggerate the importance of Washington's letter. In the many publications of the Constitution, it usually appeared as a kind of preface or introduction to the parchment. The Federalists made numerous references to it, often quoting its most persuasive passages, as happened in Massachusetts, where the Constitution faced a cloudy future. One advocate declared that Washington had "authenticated" the work of the Philadelphia convention, while another wondered how any man could oppose a political system that bore the imprint of America's greatest hero.[37] Massachusetts saw the Federalists prevail in their first great challenge. An influential polity, it was the sixth state to address ratification. Defeat of the Constitution at that juncture might have stalled, if not permanently derailed, the march to secure the nine states required to adopt the new instrument.[38]

Would Washington's commitment to the Constitution conflict with his announced intention to leave the fight for ratification to others? If he declined to attend the Virginia ratifying convention in Richmond, he knew that talented young men who were allies in the Revolution would provide effective leadership against the Antifederalist titans such as Patrick Henry and Washington's friend and Fairfax County neighbor George Mason of Gunston Hall. He had great confidence in Madison, Henry Lee, George Nicholas, and John Marshall, who eloquently and effectively defended the product of the Philadelphia assembly of notables. He may well have cringed now and then to learn that his most devoted followers at the convention, even John Marshall himself, at times minimized the consolidating potential of the Constitution. Madison, after mild optimism initially, stated that the Federalists faced an uphill battle, for prospects looked questionable if not worse by the second week of the Richmond gathering. It may surely be contended that had Virginia rejected the Constitution outright, or refused to ratify until Congress later initiated amendments, it would have eventually joined the union (which already had the required ratification of nine states), as did North Carolina in 1789 and Rhode Island in 1790. But this speculation comes with hindsight. In any case, Washington would not have been elected the first president and inaugurated in April 1789. The consequences of that fact alone are incalculable for the fortunes of the first national administration and for the future of the union itself.

Despite his initial resolution, Washington considered too much at stake to remain above the fray. Tobias Lear, Washington's private secretary, wrote to his lawyer friend William Prescott, Jr., that "the Constitution and its" prospects "have been almost the sole topics of conversation" at Mount Vernon since the struggle for its adoption began.[39] So Washington took up his pen. In the War of Independence, it proved as mighty as the sword, generating several thousand letters in behalf of unity—to Congress, state governors, and numerous other civilian and military officials to sustain the cause and further American cohesion. From his writing desk, he served as a cheerleader for the Federalist leaders. He recommended tactics to allies in several state ratifying conventions, encouraged the production of essays in defense of the Constitution, and advocated the reading of the *Federalist Papers*.[40] Maintaining that he had consumed everything he could acquire on both sides of the argument, he astutely predicted the immortality of "Publius," the pseudonym of Hamilton, Madison, and Jay, the authors of the *Federalist*. Its treatment of "freedom & the topics of government . . . will be always interesting to mankind so long as they shall be connected in Civil Society."[41] Virginia's Governor Edmund Randolph had refused to sign the Constitution in Philadelphia and now appeared uncertain of his course. Washington and Madison directly solicited the support of Randolph, who came across and helped lead the battle for approval in the ratifying convention, and Washington authorized Madison to spread the word of his "unequivocal & decided" support for the Constitution.[42] And, once again, the Circular Letter achieved high praise as required reading on the needs of the union, needs now achieved in the parchment before the state ratifying conventions. To the *Carlisle [Pa.] Gazette*, a comparison of the Circular Letter with the Constitution showed Washington's "great and comprehensive mind," surely "as enlightened in the science of government as of war."[43]

Ironically, a Washington pronouncement that generated much attention, and not a little controversy, involved the exposure of a private letter that he had wished to remain confidential. In a long missive to a fellow Virginia planter, Charles Carter, dated December 14, 1787, Washington devoted two-thirds of his remarks to agricultural experiments recently undertaken at Mount Vernon. Only then did he turn to the Constitution. His "decided opinion of the matter" was "that there is no alternative between the adoption of it and anarchy." "General Government is now suspended by a thread," he asserted. "I might go farther and say it is really at an end." As for Antifederalist criticisms, they appealed to human "passions" rather than to "reason."[44]

To Washington's embarrassment, his commentary on the Constitution and its opponents to Carter appeared later that month in the Fredericksburg *Virginia Herald*, and it eventually reached print in forty-nine newspapers. If he stood solidly behind his opinions, acknowledging that he had authorized others to repeat his general sentiments, he objected to the quoted passages on the grounds that they amounted to the "hasty and indigested production of a private letter." And yet Washington, on reflection, may have become in time less perturbed than he made out. He quickly accepted the apology of Carter, who professed that he had circulated a part of the Washington missive with the understanding that it not be given to the gazettes. Absolving Carter of any breech of confidence, Washington even begged the pardon of his Virginia friend for causing him "so much trouble."[45] Certainly Madison, although acknowledging some Antifederalist "misrepresentations" of the Carter epistle (including the claim that it was a forgery), informed Washington that he believed it to have "been of service" to the Constitution's supporters.[46]

Henry Knox displayed remarkable prescience in assessing Washington's impact on the constitutional process of 1787–1788. As he predicted, word of Washington's appointment to the Virginia delegation to the Constitutional Convention prompted other states to send their most distinguished men, who then elected Washington president of the convention. In short, Washington would give the assemblage a "national complexion" and "more than any other circumstance" lead to the ratification of "the propositions of the convention." Antifederalist James Monroe expressed the truth of Knox's prophecy when he explained the outcome to Jefferson: "Be assured . . . [Washington's] influence carried this government."[47]

Notes

1. John Adams to Samuel Osgood, Nov. 14, 1775, Smith, ed., *Letters of Delegates*, 2:342.

2. John Adams to James Warren, May 15, 1778, Smith, ed., *Letters of Delegates*, 3:678.

3. Washington to Joseph Reed, Jan. 31, 1776, Washington to Joseph Reed, April 1, 1776, Washington to John Augustine Washington, May 31–[June 4], 1776, *GW Papers: Rev. War Ser.*, 3:228, 4:11, 411–12. Washington also told Reed that *Common Sense* "is working a powerful change . . . in the Minds of many Men" in Virginia. *GW Papers: Rev. War Ser.*, 3:228, 4:11.

4. Washington to John Hancock, July 10, 1776, General Orders, July 9, 1776, *GW Papers: Rev. War Ser.*, 5:258, 246; James Thomas Flexner, *George Washington*, 4 vols. (New York, 1965–1972), 2:97. Since the original of Washington's General Orders has not survived, the editors of *GW Papers: Rev. War. Ser.* used the copy in the so-called Varick transcripts, where the words Country and State are capitalized. Though spelling and capitalization were far from standardized in the eighteenth century, Washington himself normally capitalized these words.

5. Don Higginbotham, *George Washington and the American Military Tradition* (Athens, Ga., 1985).

6. Fred W. Anderson, "The Hinge of the Revolution: George Washington Confronts a People's Army, July 3, 1775," *Massachusetts Historical Review*, 1 (1999), 45; *GW Papers: Rev. War. Ser.*, 1:54.

7. Anderson, "Hinge of the Revolution," 21–48; Higginbotham, *Washington and the American Military Tradition*, chaps. 1–2. The issue of Massachusetts soldiers' pay schedule is in *GW Papers: Rev. War Ser.*, 2:456–57, 502–03.

8. *GW Papers: Rev. War Ser.*, 1:459.

9. Paul F. Boller, Jr., *Washington and Religion* (Dallas, Tex., 1963), 124–36, quotation on p. 126.

10. Washington to the president of Congress, June 8, 1777, *GW Papers: Rev. War. Ser.*, 9:644–45.

11. *GW Papers: Rev. War. Ser.*, 2:331, 335, 3:3–4.

12. Washington to Richard Peters, April 17, 1777, *GW Papers: Rev. War. Ser.*, 9:196.

13. This paragraph draws particularly on Charles P. Neimeyer, *America Goes to War: A Social History of the Continental Army* (New York, 1996); Don Higginbotham, "The American Militia: A Traditional Institution with Revolutionary Responsibilities," *Reconsiderations on the Revolutionary War: Selected Essays*, ed. Higginbotham (Westport, Conn., and London, 1978), 83–103; Charles H. Lesser, *The Sinews of Independence: Monthly Strength Reports of the Continental Army* (Chicago, 1976); and Holly A. Mayer, *Belonging to the Army: Camp Followers and Community during the American Revolution* (Columbia, S.C., 1996), quotation on p. ix.

14. Don Higginbotham, *Daniel Morgan: Revolutionary Rifleman* (Chapel Hill, N.C., 1961), 95–99. General Nathanael Greene stated that General George Weedon's Virginia brigade saved the American army from disaster at the Battle of Brandywine on September 11, 1777. But Washington never singled the brigade out for praise because they were from his own state. Greene to Henry Marchant, July [25], 1778, Richard K. Showman et al., eds., *The Papers of General Nathanael Greene*, 10 vols. to date (Chapel Hill, N.C., 1976–), 2:471.

15. John Marshall, *An Autobiographical Sketch*, ed. John Stokes Adams (Ann Arbor, Mich., 1937), 9–10. See also Marshall's remarks on the Revolutionary officer corps in his *The Life of George Washington*, 5 vols. (Philadelphia, 1804–1807), 2:71–72, 77.

16. John C. Dann, ed., *The Revolution Remembered: Eyewitness Accounts of the War for Independence* (Chicago and London, 1980), 62. Lawrence Babits informs me that, after reading hundreds of Revolutionary War veterans' pension applications, he was struck by the large number of former soldiers who made reference to having named sons after George Washington.

17. "Farewell Orders to the Armies of the United States," Nov. 2, 1783, John C. Fitzpatrick, ed., *The Writings of George Washington . . .*, 39 vols. (Washington, D.C., 1931–1944), 27:224 (hereafter cited as *GW Writings*).

18. Royster, *A Revolutionary People*, chaps. 6–8. Just how far some officers (mostly at the field-grade level) were prepared to go, acting

against Congress or the states, or both, is still in dispute. For an analysis of the lengthy secondary literature, see Higginbotham, *Washington and the American Military Tradition*, 156–57.

19. Volumes 1–3 of *GW Papers: Rev. War Ser.* contain fifty-one letters to the president of Congress, thirty-four to the Massachusetts legislature, forty to Governor Jonathan Trumbull of Connecticut, and thirty to Governor Nicholas Cooke of Rhode Island.

20. *GW Papers: Rev. War Ser.*, 5:256–57.

21. *GW Writings*, 11:291–92.

22. Sentiments on a Peace Establishment, *GW Writings*, 26:374–98.

23. Circular to the States, June 1783, *GW Writings*, 24:483–96.

24. Washington to Henry Knox, Dec. 26, 1786, W. W. Abbot et al., eds., *The Papers of George Washington: Confederation Series*, 6 vols. (Charlottesville, Va., 1992–1997), 4:481–84, quotation on p. 482 (hereafter cited as *GW Papers: Conf. Ser.*).

25. *GW Papers: Conf. Ser.*, 4:481–84, 481, 483.

26. Priestly quoted in Adair, *Fame and the Founding Fathers*, 117; Washington to David Stuart, Nov. 30, 1785, *GW Papers: Conf. Ser.*, 3:423.

27. Max Farrand, ed., *Records of the Federal Convention of 1787*, 4 vols. (New Haven, Conn., 1911–1937), 2:642–43.

28. John M. Murrin, "War, Revolution, and Nation-Making: The American Revolution versus the Civil War," 9, an unpublished paper cited with the author's permission.

29. Jacob E. Cooke, ed., *The Federalist* (Middletown, Conn., 1961), 594.

30. Washington to Henry Lee, April 4, 1786, *GW Papers: Conf. Ser.*, 4:4. A fuller account of Washington's part in constitutional reform is Don Higginbotham, "George Washington's Contributions to American Constitutionalism," in Higginbotham, *War and Society in Revolutionary America: The Wider Dimensions of Conflict* (Columbia, S.C., 1988), 193–213.

31. Merrill Jensen, John P. Kaminski, Gaspare J. Saladino et al., eds., *The Documentary History of the Ratification of the Constitution*, 16 vols. to date (Madison, Wis. 1976–), 13:60–61 (hereafter cited as *Documentary History Ratification*).

32. Washington to Madison, March 31, 1787, Madison to Washington, April 16, 1787, "Notes on the Sentiments on the Government of John Jay, Henry Knox, and James Madison," [c. April 1787], GW Papers: Conf. Ser., 5:114–17, 144–50, 163–66; Stuart Leibiger, Founding Friendship: George Washington, James Madison, and the Creation of the American Republic (Charlottesville, Va., 1999), chap. 3.

33. Glen A. Phelps, George Washington & American Constitutionalism (Lawrence, Kan., 1993), 82, 92–95, provides a useful summary of Washington's conflicted feelings about attending the Philadelphia convention.

34. Though rarely speaking on the floor of the convention, even when he stepped down as president and the delegates debated as a committee of the whole, there is evidence that Washington adhered to a strongly nationalist position, siding with Madison on issues where his views can be identified. Phelps, Washington and American Constitutionalism, 102–11; Arthur N. Holcombe, "The Role of Washington in the Framing of the Constitution," Huntington Library Quarterly, 19 (1956), 317–34; William B. Allen, "Washington and Franklin: Symbols or Lawmakers," Political Science Reviewer, 17 (1987), 122–27; Leibiger, Founding Friendship, 70–83.

35. "It is one of the evils perhaps not the smallest, of democratical Governments that the People must feel before they will see or act" to reform their constitutions. Washington to David Humphreys, Washington to Henry Knox, both March 8, 1787, Washington to John Jay, March 10, 1787, GW Papers: Conf. Ser., 5:73, 74–75, 79–80, quotation in slightly varying language in all letters.

36. Washington to the president of Congress, Sept. 17, 1787, GW Papers: Conf. Ser., 5:330–31. In April, a month or so before the Philadelphia convention opened, Madison had called for such a letter to explain any subsequent changes in the constitutional structure of the nation: "An explanatory address must of necessity accompany the result of the Convention on the main objective." Madison to Edmund Randolph, April 8, 1787, in William T. Hutchinson, Robert A. Rutland, J. C. A. Stagg et al., eds., The Papers of James Madison, Congressional Series, 17 vols. (Chicago and Charlottesville, Va., 1962–1991), 9:369.

37. *Documentary History Ratification*, 6:1417, 4:85. For other examples from Massachusetts, see *Documentary History Ratification*, 4:57, 84–85, 107, 272, 292, 250, 584.

38. Jackson Turner Main, *The Antifederalists: Critics of the Constitution, 1781–1788* (Chapel Hill, N.C., 1961), 200–10. "Here lay the decisive conflict; had the Constitution lost in Massachusetts, it would never have been ratified." Main, *The Antifederalists*, 210. See also Michael Allen Gillespie, "Massachusetts: Creating Consensus," *Ratifying the Constitution*, eds. Michael Allen Gillespie and Michael Lienesch (Lawrence, Kan., 1989), 138–67.

39. *Documentary History Ratification*, 16:307.

40. Washington to Lafayette, Sept. 18, 1787, Washington to David Humphreys, Oct. 10, 1787, Washington to David Stuart, Oct. 17, Nov. 5, 30, 1787, Washington to Thomas Johnson, April 20, 1788, Washington to James McHenry, April 27, 1788, Washington to Charles Cotesworth Pinckney, June 28, 1788, *GW Papers: Conf. Ser.*, 5:334, 365–66, 379–80, 411–12, 466–67, 6:217–18, 234–35, 361–63.

41. Washington to Alexander Hamilton, Aug. 28, 1788, *GW Papers: Conf. Ser.*, 6:481. "Though Washington often spoke highly of the *Federalist Papers* as they were being published . . . this is his most expansive expression of praise." *GW Papers: Conf. Ser.*, 6:482 n2.

42. Washington to Edmund Randolph, Jan. 8, 1788, Washington to Madison, Jan. 10, 1788, *GW Papers: Conf. Ser.*, 6:17–18, 32–33.

43. *Documentary History Ratification*, 13:61–62.

44. Washington to Charles Carter, Dec. 14, 1787, *GW Papers: Conf. Ser.*, 5:489–92.

45. Washington to Charles Carter, Jan. 12, 20, 22, 1788, *GW Papers: Conf. Ser.*, 6: 37, 48, 53. Still another Washington letter, written to Caleb Gibbs of Masachusetts on Feb. 29, 1788, was printed in all thirteen states, a total of fifty times. Washington had no objection to its appearance in the press. It predicted that Virginia would approve the Constitution. *Documentary History Ratification*, 16:464–65.

46. Madison to Washington, Feb. 20, 1788, in Hutchinson et al., eds., *Madison Papers*, 10:527. See also *Documentary History Ratification*, 15:135–43.

47. Henry Knox to Washington, March 19, 1787, *GW Papers: Conf. Ser.*, 5:96–97; Julian P. Boyd et al., eds., *The Papers of Thomas Jefferson*, 28 vols. to date (Princeton, N.J., 1951–), 13:351–52.

CHAPTER THREE

∽

The Unifier as President

Was Washington equally a unifying influence as president? That was his intention; it explains why he accepted an office that the framers seemingly created with him in mind as its first occupant. Though reluctant to return to public life owing to his 1783 promise not to serve in office again, to advancing age, and to so many years away from family and home during the Revolutionary War, he came to recognize that his country expected him to do so, as is evidenced by the torrent of his incoming mail. His correspondents either urged him to accept the presidency or, more often, assumed he had no choice but to do so.[1] He knew that the Constitution alone would not guarantee acceptance of the political system, especially one that was new and untried, and one that, in this case, had been ratified in the face of substantial opposition, with two states still outside the pale when Washington took his presidential oath. Losers in such contests do not always accept the verdict. And it remained problematic as Washington launched his administration whether the Antifederalists would cross over and support the government.

Moreover, as much as Washington favored the republican approach to nation-making contained in the Constitution, he knew that republics tended to short, turbulent life spans, a reflection that men were flawed creatures whose passions and narrow self-interests could not easily be contained within the bounds of law and constitutions. Washington and his fellow constitution-makers at Philadelphia had doubly flown in the face of history by also creating a vast, continental republic, the kind that appeared most likely to quickly self-destruct. A nation on such a huge scale, with a multitude of interests and attitudes, posed an enormous challenge for Washington the Unifier. In his first inaugural address, he warned his countrymen that "the destiny of the Republican model of Government" rested in their hands.[2]

Seymour Martin Lipset writes that "all new nations and post-revolutionary societies" face a "crisis of legitimacy." When the imperial power is defeated or otherwise acknowledges independence of former colonies, sentiment for union is likely to decline without a common danger. What is particularly lacking is tradition, which is highly visible in older countries with deep-seated monarchical values and beliefs. In such situations, leaders such as Washington can make a difference, and he did. To the Antifederalists, who retained their trust and confidence in Washington, he helped give legitimacy to the Constitution and the new government that took office in 1789. Gouverneur Morris, the facile penman who had shaped the final draft of the Constitution, predicted that result when he wrote Washington that "You alone can awe the Insolence of opposing Factions & the greater Insolence of assuming Adherents. . . . You will become a Father to more than three Millions of Children."[3] That Washington would do so must have been the fervent belief of the thousands who turned out to cheer and praise him on his journey from Virginia to the capital of New York City that year, an outpouring of tribute and affection that must have been unparalleled in the western world of that time.[4]

As president, Washington devoted great attention to his cere-monial role as head of state. That included sitting for portraits, a practice at which he was already well versed from posing for six artists over the years. He patiently did so for over a dozen more during his presidency. Although they may not have added to his stature and authority, they surely reinforced it. "In the late eigh-teenth century, portraits played a significant role in recalling a person's character as well as appearance, because it was believed that a person's face revealed his or her mental and emotional characteristics."[5] Some resulted from requests from public groups such as the Boston selectmen, who sought his likeness to hang in Faneuil Hall; others came from institutions such as Harvard Col-lege, which requested that the president sit for artist Edward Sav-age, so that he could create an image to adorn Philosophical Hall. Washington agreed to various other requests for likenesses to hang in New York City Hall and in the city council chambers of Charleston, South Carolina, but the constraints of time led him to courteously reject others—his three sittings for Edward Savage had taken seven hours.

Washington must have agreed with the words of James Wilson at the Constitutional Convention that the president, renouncing local and regional ties, would impartially watch over the nation. Washington knew he must remain above divisive issues in Con-gress, and he must eschew affiliation with any faction or party and avoid emphasizing his membership in Freemasonry and the Society of the Cincinnati since both were controversial in some quarters, especially the Cincinnati. Otherwise, he could not ef-fectively urge the American people to identify with America, nor could he impress on the states the supremacy of national juris-diction.[6]

One way of accomplishing these objectives was the issuing of proclamations of various kinds and the giving of annual state of the union messages in the name of the nation. Perhaps because Washington lacked an easy familiarity of manner, we have not adequately appreciated his recognition of the importance of both the spoken and the written word. In delivering his messages in person, he reinforced his identity with the government, in speeches that were written carefully, sometimes the product of several drafts. The use of a prepared text conveyed the impression that the president was thoughtful and serious, worthy of the close attention of his countrymen. It was Washington, and future presidents as well, who spoke to the people and for the people, not the Congress or the Judiciary. In attaching his name to public documents and other important writings, Washington parted company with some republican thinkers such as Jefferson, who continued to favor the self-effacement of leaders and the assertion of "principles over men." According to this view, the reputation or standing of texts should come from their content, not their authors. (Jefferson's authorship of the Declaration of Independence was still little known before the 1790s.)[7]

Another way of getting the citizenry to identify with him as president and with the national government was to see him in the flesh. Senator William McClay of Pennsylvania voiced the need to do so, as well as its possible pitfalls: "General Washington stood on as difficult Ground, as he had ever done in his life. That to suffer himself to be run down on the one hand by a Croud of Visitants so as to engross his time would never do. . . . But on the other hand for him to be seen only in public on Stated times like an Eastern lama would be equally offensive." During the first year of his presidency, while the government resided in New York City, Washington hosted Thursday evening dinners, limited to about a dozen guests (the number that could be seated around his dining table). His intention was eventually to include all members of Congress, foreign diplomats, and other important officials. As chief executive he celebrated at his mansion New Year's Day and Independence Day, events which became a presidential tradition lasting into the twentieth century. Naturally reserved though he was, the president frequently left his house and encountered ordinary people on his regular walks down to the Battery and when he took in the circus and other amusements.[8]

On the national level, Washington wanted his countrymen to encounter *their* president, a man interested in learning their views on issues, a man free of regional or local biases. In the fall of 1789, having pledged to visit every state, an unbelievably arduous undertaking in that day, he set off for Connecticut, Massachusetts, and New Hampshire. Large, enthusiastic crowds greeted him everywhere, but none pricked his emotions more than in Boston. As he recorded in his diary, "we came to the State House; from which, across the Street, an Arch was thrown; in front of which was this Inscription—'To the Man who unites all hearts' and on the other—'To Columbia's favourite Son.'" The following year he returned to New England, this time to Rhode Island, which had only recently ratified the Constitution. North Carolina, the other state to delay joining hands until after he became president, drew his immediate attention. He sought to tie this tardy state even more securely to the rest. He displayed that motive in choosing for a Supreme Court seat James Iredell of North Carolina, "a State of some importance in the Union," which thus far had none of its citizens occupying "a federal Office." He toured that state and all of its southern neighbors in 1791, a trek of nearly 2,000 miles. During his week-long stay in Charleston, South Carolina, he rode the length of the city to cheering crowds, attended seven formal dinners, drank sixty toasts, danced at a ball, observed a fireworks display, visited an orphanage, and examined Revolutionary War battle sites. Arduous though they were, his journeys constituted high political drama. And everywhere he preached the gospel of a forceful new national identity.[9]

On these and other occasions, Washington held out the hand of reconciliation to former Loyalists and Antifederalists. During the Revolutionary War itself he had strenuously discouraged patriot groups from taking the law into their own

hands and avoiding the judicial process against the king's supporters. The family he had been closest to from his youth, the
Fairfaxes, sat out the war; that included his influential bene-
factor, Thomas, Lord Fairfax, proprietor of the Northern Neck,
and Bryan Fairfax, with whom Washington exchanged heated,
although polite, epistles as to the meaning of the mounting crisis with Britain before Lexington and Concord. Bryan's brother
George William and his wife Sally had an endearing relationship with George and Martha Washington before they traveled
to England in 1773, never to return, although at the end of the
conflict Washington informed them of his ardent wish that
they again reside in Virginia. After 1783 Washington resumed
his correspondence with various British friends and acquaintances and formed other rewarding relationships by letter as
well. He backed the full implementation of the treaty of peace,
which provided for an end to mistreatment of the Loyalists and
recommended to the states to take a number of generous steps,
such as to allow those crown adherents who had not committed crimes or made war on the United States to return to
America and to permit real British citizens to regain their con-
fiscated estates.

The commander in chief sent a significant message to any patriots bent on vengeance against the Loyalists when he marched
into New York City after General Guy Carleton's British troops
evacuated that urban center in late November 1783, ending a
seven-year occupation. Disbanding most of his army, Washington
entered Manhattan with a trusted body of veterans who could be
counted on to maintain law and order. His aide, Colonel Benjamin Tallmadge, recalled that "not one instance occurred of any
abuse, after we took possession of the city, where protection was
given or engaged." Somehow, during that busy week, Washington
displayed the time and willingness to respond to an appeal by an
ardent Loyalist, Judge Andrew Elliot, who had written from a
vessel of the British evacuation fleet in the harbor. Washington

responded that, as requested, he had checked on the welfare of Elliot's daughter in the city and offered the lady any assistance she might need.[10]

Washington could be especially forgiving of trimmers or people who saw themselves as neutralists and who eventually joined, nominally at least, the Revolutionary side during the war. He replied positively to the Reverend William Smith, former provost of the College of Philadelphia, and now rector of a new college on the Maryland Eastern Shore that bore Washington's name. Flattered by the naming, he contributed money to the school and later received an honorary degree. In 1776, Smith had written a pamphlet attacking Paine's *Common Sense* and also penned several articles against independence. Although as president Washington appointed few men to federal office suspected of loyalism or identified as such, a notable exception was Tench Coxe, who became Alexander Hamilton's principal assistant in the Treasury Department. After fleeing to British-held territory in 1776, Coxe avoided arrest when the king's army evacuated Philadelphia in 1778 by taking an oath of allegiance.[11]

Thus Washington contributed significantly to what was a strikingly different ending to most civil wars and revolutionary insurrections in modern history. The winners in such struggles have more often than not turned to purges and/or trials against their "morally freighted" countrymen. Washington recognized as well or better than any other American that, as scholars are increasingly finding, thousands of Americans did not act consistently for one side or the other. Rather than dramatic shifts in allegiance—few could be called Benedict Arnolds—they displayed ambivalence, a concern to shelter their locality (whichever side controlled it), and a desire to protect themselves. Evidence shows, for example, that not uncommonly Continental soldiers captured by the British then served in the royal forces, and ended up again in Revolutionary service after being recaptured or deserting.[12]

As for the Antifederalists, Washington reached out to them in various ways. He continued on very good terms with the Antifederalist governor of New York, George Clinton, an old friend. He dined with Clinton the night he arrived in New York City for his inauguration as president. During the next few days Washington appears to have gone out of his way to be seen in the company of the governor, quite possibly as a gesture to the recent opponents of the Constitution that Americans should come together and bury their once-heated political differences. The new president even initiated a revival of his friendship with Patrick Henry, the leader of Virginia Antifederalism, in 1795. Within twelve months or so, he offered Henry three different federal offices. Though Henry declined to accept in each case, he expressed deep appreciation. An earlier political reconciliation with Samuel Chase of Maryland, another foe of the Constitution initially, resulted in the president's appointing Chase to the Supreme Court in 1796. The Marylander had come over to the president's view of the new national charter.[13] Washington acknowledged soon after Virginia's ratification of the Constitution that the opponents in the Old Dominion, "as in most of the other States, have conducted themselves with great prudence & political moderation." They had expressed some concerns at least worthy of consideration. He knew that the absence of a bill of rights in the Constitution had been the most effective rallying cry of the Antifederalists, many of whom were "respectable characters and well meaning men."[14]

Consequently, in virtually the only specific recommendation for legislative action in his first inaugural, he urged Congress to address the question of amendments, which, as he reminded the members, the Constitution authorized in Article V. In a substantial paragraph of his speech (it fills a little more than four printed pages), he expressed confidence that the lawmakers could review the subject of what ought to be "the characteristic rights of freemen" in the context of a concern for the future "public harmony" of the country. A short time later he responded to Madison's personal appeal to provide him a letter in support of the Virginia congressman's proposed rights amendments, which seemed to be making little headway since the House of Representatives had thus far at best showed indifference to them. "Upon the whole," wrote Washington, "they have my wishes for a favourable reception in both houses." Stuart Leibiger, a leading authority, is convinced that "without Washington's help, Madison's crusade for what has become a constitutional cornerstone would have been hopeless."[15] A related result of Washington's involvement, his prediction to Governor Samuel Johnston of North Carolina that a bill of rights would be adopted and ratified, received wide publicity and enthusiastic approval in that state before its second ratification convention endorsed the Constitution in late 1789.[16] Indeed, it is hard to escape the conclusion that Congress, on agreeing to recommend the amendments that became the Bill of Rights, deliberately linked them to Washington's name: the lawmakers requested *him* to transmit copies of the proposed amendments to the executives of the eleven states then in the union and to those of North Carolina and Rhode Island as well.[17]

In still other ways Washington sought to bring people together. He did so concerning religion. It had also been true in the Revolution, but now he could reach a larger audience and have a greater influence. It was easier to do than it might have been for other leaders because he genuinely believed in religious freedom. Unlike certain other areas, where he sought to speak for the nation, he did not wish to address the American people on personal questions of faith, but he voiced his respect for all denominations and thus did his part to keep a subject that divided people the world over then (and still does today) from weakening the ties of nationhood. After his first inaugural, he exchanged salutations with 22 major religious groups. In these and other communications with such bodies, he praised religion in general terms, without expressing a preference for certain creeds. He continued his practice, dating from the Revolution and continuing at the Constitutional Convention, of attending the services of various denominations, including Congregational, Lutheran, Dutch Reform, and Roman Catholic. He also occasionally contributed to building funds of some churches. In these sanctuaries, he told the Jews of Newport, Rhode Island, they should feel comfortable as Americans. "May the Children of the Stock of Abraham, who dwell in this land, continue to merit and enjoy the good will of the other Inhabitants; while every one shall sit in safety under his own vine and fig tree, and there shall be none to make him afraid."[18] (To maintain this aura of impartiality to faiths, as well as to friends and public officials, Washington decided not to attend private funerals as president.)[19]

Washington's speeches, proclamations, travels, visits to churches, sittings for artists, and exchanges of salutations with religious and governmental groups reveal a chief executive keenly aware that his ceremonial responsibilities, like his public policy actions, enhanced his visibility and symbolic stature for the new nation. His frequent attendance at the theater not only had the impact of promoting drama in the country but also delivered a message against intolerance, as had his pronouncements to Jews, Catholics, and other minorities. Even before becoming president, he had attended a play in Philadelphia at a time when state law still prohibited theatrical activity, purchasing four "Play Tickets" to see a performance by Lewis Hallam, Jr., and other actors of the American Company. Quite likely Washington helped lessen the influence of evangelicals and other sects against the stage in America.[20]

In all this, according to John Adams, Washington played superbly the actor's role. The statement, though true, does not convict Washington of insincerity. As a public figure, he had long been sensitive to the meaningful word or gesture or timing of an act—his wearing his Virginia militia uniform at the Second Continental Congress, his appearance before disgruntled army officers at Newburgh (he spoke of growing gray and almost blind in the service of his country), his speech before Congress in surrendering his commission as commander in chief at the close of the War of Independence, his well-publicized hesitancy before agreeing to attend the Constitutional Convention, and, afterward, to accept the presidency, his kissing the Bible (not called for in the Constitution) after the presidential oath, his riding at the head of the militia force that marched against the Pennsylvania whiskey rebels, and his Farewell Address. "These were all in a strain of Shakespearean and Garrickal excellence in dramatic exhibitions."[21]

Adams, Washington's vice president, had known his chief up close for twenty-five years, and yet he hardly understood how to comprehend the man, seeming to question whether Washington actually recognized the significance of his flair for the stage. Thus he made no real effort to do so in the retrospective years of old age when he labored over his autobiography. Moreover, Washington hagiography had reached the point where Adams could never cut his way through the thicket of cherry trees and Godlike virtue and wisdom. Adams, in language of a later day, normally shot from the hip. To the modern ear, his candor is refreshing; in his own time it spelled no end of political trouble. But Adams made Washington his exception. He kept his feelings about the Virginian bottled up except for such Thespian references in private correspondence to Dr. Benjamin Rush and other trusted friends. In those missives he made it abundantly clear that he felt that the adulation of Washington by Parson Weems, John Marshall, and others was unhealthy for the country and, implicitly, denigrated other Revolutionary leaders who had made significant contributions to the new nation. A painfully honest man, Adams put himself high on that list. Even so, in moments of cool reflection, Adams admitted that Washington ranked first among founders in integrity and service. Adams, a man who knew he talked too much, probably admired most Washington's "gift of silence . . . one of the most precious talents."[22]

Of course, there were Washington critics. Naysayers contended that, among other things, some of his doings smacked of kingship, an example being George and Martha Washington's "republican court." The term refers to their regularly scheduled social gatherings: the president's, open to the public (males only) on Tuesdays, and the first lady's, by invitation, for both sexes on Fridays. With the encouragement of her husband, Martha's drawing room, writes David Shields, became the center for a new republican style of conversation and sociability over lemonade, tea, cake, and ice cream. The republican court sought to bring people together from different parts of the country, with one intended result to moderate divisions in Congress. In this atmosphere, an unattached lawmaker might, with the help of Martha Washington, land a highly desirable spouse. The president's lady brokered sixteen marriages, including that of James Madison and Dolley Payne. The republican court "contributed greatly to the consolidation of a governing class interrelated on a continental scale." In this open, informal atmosphere, refined women felt free to instruct "public men in manners, morality, and policy."[23]

Another benefit of the republican court, however intended, gave women a greater sense of equality with men. The Washingtons, it would seem, did not fully subscribe to the allegedly dominant idea in American life of fixed gender spaces of activity.[24] As for the president's own role, Abigail Adams, wife of the former minister to the Court of St. James, observed that Washington made it a point to engage every lady in individual conversation at Martha's levees. He did so "with a grace, dignity & ease, that leaves Royal George far behind him." And on those Friday gatherings he left behind the sword that he wore and the hat that he carried during his Tuesday receptions. The levees were Martha's, and he appeared as a private citizen. The republican court did not survive in the Jeffersonian presidency, partly because the master of Monticello failed to share George and Martha Washington's views on the empowerment of women. Still, the republican court played a constructive role in the formative period of national consolidation.[25]

At social affairs and other functions, Washington came to know members of Congress from the newly created states of Vermont, Kentucky, and Tennessee. When he spoke of the nation, he had always meant more than the original thirteen states. He had included the vast western regions extending to the Mississippi River. W. W. Abbot states the matter well: the West first stretched Washington's mind beyond his native Virginia. His association with that domain, "more than anything else, except the war itself, served to prepare him for the role of nation builder."[26] Washington knew more about the trans-Appalachian domain than any other American leader. He journeyed into the Ohio country several times, first in 1753 as Virginia's emissary to order the French out of the long-disputed region. He had defended Virginia's extensive borderlands in the French and Indian War. By the 1780s he owned thousands of acres in the interior. Both before and after the Revolution he had explored its rivers, bottomlands, and valleys. In 1783, he boasted to the French military veteran and philosophe, François Jean Chastellux, of the unlimited possibilities for the "inland navigation of these united States . . . & could not but be struck with the immense diffusion & importance of it." The "western Country" had "given bounds to a new Empire." And the following year, as he suggested to Richard Henry Lee, at the time president of the Confederation Congress, "all Mines, Minerals & Salt Springs" found in the public domain should be set aside for the benefit of the nation so that they would not be monopolized by "the few knowing ones": speculators and other land jobbers.[27]

But this gigantic resource, the West, should be tied firmly to the original states: it had the potential to enrich the union by bolstering the economy, serving as a "safety valve," as Frederick Jackson Turner phrased it, for people seeking new homes and fresh opportunities, and further knotting together the original states because of their common stake in the West. At the same time, if the central government could not maintain law and order in the frontier areas and develop inland transportation by means of rivers and canals (and here he included the interior portions of the older states), the settlers would become "alienated," feeling as "unconnected with us" as "we are with South America"; and they would likely ally themselves with Britain or Spain. If there were such a division "between the Eastern & Western Country," the consequences might "be fatal" to the nation.[28]

With good reason, Washington voiced these alarms. In 1789, as he entered office, threatening reports arrived at the nation's capital. George Nicholas, a recent émigré to Kentucky, confided to his friend James Madison what might happen if his "expectations from the justice and policy of the new Government" met with disappointment; "that government which with-holds from us the necesssary defence and suffers our most valuable rights to be taken away from us by another nation has no right to expect our support."[29] This private opinion received reinforcement from a more influential source: Arthur St. Clair, governor of the Northwest Territory. In a letter that fills ten pages in the Washington *Presidential Series*, St. Clair warned that western settlers, with England and Spain on their northern and southern borders, "will be exposed to the Machinations of both" and "might be tempted to throw off all Connection with the Parent States."[30]

These concerns explain Washington's determination to act decisively against Indian tribes north of the Ohio River and to resolve problems about the Northwest with Britain and about the Southwest with Spain. Two military expeditions under Josiah Harmar and Arthur St. Clair suffered defeat at the hands of the tribesmen, but a larger, better equipped and officered army, under General Anthony Wayne, won a decisive victory at the Battle of Fallen Timbers in 1794. The subsequent Treaty of Greenville paved the way for a wave of new settlers on the frontier and the admission of Ohio as a state into the union a few years later. As one historian points out, pioneers in the Ohio Valley had little sense of national structures in the 1790s. The most tangible instrument was Anthony Wayne's victorious army.[31] The Jay Treaty with Britain in 1794 led to the removal of British garrisons at Detroit and elsewhere along the Great Lakes, and the following year the Pinckney Treaty with Spain opened the Mississippi River to western farmers so that they could use that waterway to exit their produce by New Orleans and into the Gulf of Mexico.

The mid-1790s found Washington reacting to another problem of order and stability. He acted decisively in 1794 against the whiskey rebels of western Pennsylvania, where he used federalized militia to enforce a controversial tax on distillers. Here is another example of Washington's attaching himself—that is, his enormous prestige—to an act of the national government, for he personally took the field at the head of the 13,000-man militia army, the only time in American history that a president has led the militia in the field. This successful upholding of federal law, according to Washington, demonstrated "the most conclusive refutation that could have been given to the assertions of Lord Sheffield" on the American future "and the predictions of others of his cast, that without the protection of G. Britain, we should be unable to govern ourselves; and would soon be involved in anarchy and confusion."[32]

Another and more serious source of divisiveness than the Whiskey Rebellion, one that made Washington's second term something of a nightmare, was the international impact of the French Revolution, a development that spawned the "confusion" he feared. If the president desired to be neutral himself in the face of internal political discord, he wished for himself and the country neutrality on the world scene as well. On the eve of the upheaval in France, he affirmed his hope that America "will be able to keep disengaged from the labyrinth of European politics & Wars."[33] Though he had valued the French alliance during the War of Independence, he remained mindful, as he had told Henry

Laurens, president of the Continental Congress in 1778, that Gallic ties could create difficulties in the future if some Americans developed "an excess of confidence in France." He felt that the French alliance—or any alliance for that matter—effectively lasted only so long as it met the national interest of the signatories.[34] When the French Revolution in the early 1790s turned increasing violent and led to a rapidly escalating European war, Washington concluded that the alliance no longer met America's interests, that it indeed constituted a danger since the country could be sucked into a conflict that would damage a young nation preoccupied with tightening the bonds of nationality.

The president knew from experience that wars usually fracture people rather than unite them. Military conflict, "this plague to Mankind," he exclaimed, should be "banished from the Earth" so that mankind could be employed in more valuable pursuits than those that lead to "the destruction of the human race."[35] (Had he been privy to later American history, he would have found that only in the two World Wars of the twentieth century have conflicts served to unite the American people.) Consequently, he issued his so-called Neutrality Proclamation in 1793, which in its wording failed to satisfy his principal ministers, the pro-British Hamilton and the pro-French Jefferson. Two years later he signed the Jay Treaty with England that pleased virtually no one, but it avoided a clash over long-standing issues and did achieve some successes. The military posts, which Britain previously failed to relinquish following the Revolutionary War and now agreed to evacuate, had been a painful reminder to Washington, the champion of American territorial integrity, that a nation is hardly sovereign if foreign troops occupy its soil and it can do nothing about it. Moreover, the country had avoided a European conflict, partly because he had neither acted nor spoken in a provocative manner in dealing with Britain, and he had voiced restraint to Congress. "The Constitution," as Washington noted in a different context, "vests the power of declaring war with Congress," which have to deliberate "on the subject, and authorize such a measure."[36]

Washington spoke correctly in contending that foreign relations, especially war with a European power, presented the gravest threat to the American union during his presidency. For further evidence of that, he could have pointed to extremist threats resulting from Southerners' attempt to impose economic penalties on the British. Northerners generally objected to them because of the importance of British investments in the country and their substantial payments of customs duties. Vice President John Adams averred that the continent was now divided along North-South sectional lines. Senator Rufus King of New York warned John Taylor of Virginia that the Northeastern states felt increasingly alienated from the South.[37] Toward the end of his administration, Washington reminded Patrick Henry that to favor either England or France would "create dissensions, disturb the public tranquility, and destroy, perhaps for ever the cement which binds the Union."[38] Various Federalist writers contended that Washington, not the Constitution, held the country together in that decade.[39] Washington would not have been entirely pleased with such flattering words, for he foresaw that, in the years that lay ahead, it would be the legal foundation of the country, not the lengthened shadow of a single man, or a succession of men, that would determine America's fate. Even so, Washington, writes Glen Phelps, "viewed the president as having a special guardianship of the Constitution," one that he came to share with the federal judiciary as a result of the nature of his appointments.[40]

Washington played his own part in the growth of the Supreme Court as a voice for the rule of law at a time when questions involving opposition to the whiskey excise, the loyalty of Westerners, and foreign policy tensions created concerns about national cohesion. His appointees to the high bench never faltered in their commitment to the union and to the Constitution as the highest law of the land. Aware that some Americans feared that the federal judiciary, including the district and appellate levels, would become an agency of oppression, Washington sought to dissipate those feelings "by making appointments to the federal bench from the citizens of the state where the courts sat and by deliberately seeking geographical representation on the Supreme Court." Moreover, Washington nominated able men to the high court, such as John Jay, James Wilson, James Iredell, and Oliver Ellsworth. As early as the 1790s, the judiciary took on the function of the "nation's schoolmaster," especially in the justices' grand jury charges, which were published in the newspapers, and which became catechisms of constitutional primacy and of the sacred character of the union.[41] None outdid Justice Iredell. A greatly strengthened union under the Constitution, he once intoned, has "enabled us to reach our present envied situation, so, under the blessing of God, nothing but Disunion can in all human probability deprive us of it!"[42]

The high bench has never had a greater admirer of Washington and his concept of nationhood than John Marshall, a fellow Virginian, who in 1784 exclaimed that Washington ranked as "the greatest Man on earth."[43] A Washington protégé, he served as a Continental officer, advocate for ratifying the Constitution, supporter of the Washington administration in the 1790s, and author of a five-volume biography of the first president. In the House of Representatives at the time of Washington's death, Marshall delivered that body's eulogy, ending with the famous words: "First in war, First in Peace, First in the hearts of his countrymen," which, as Marshall always acknowledged, were contributed to him by Henry Lee. Marshall also co-chaired Congress's funeral arrangements, led the procession through the streets of Philadelphia, and introduced the bill for a monument to the deceased ex-president in the District of Columbia, the new capital.[44] "No one in public life had been closer to Washington in his final years," observes Marshall biographer Jean Edward

Smith, who also reminds us that in chronicling Washington's career, Marshall wrote about his mentor and the union "as if they were inseparable."[45] As chief justice of the Supreme Court from 1801 to 1835, Marshall's nationalist opinions continued Washington's work of putting flesh on the Constitution and preaching the gospel of union.[46]

Notes

1. W. W. Abbot et al., eds., *The Papers of George Washington: Presidential Series*, 11 vols. to date (Charlottesville, Va., 1987–), vols. 1–2, throughout (hereafter cited as *GW Papers: Pres. Ser.*).

2. First Inaugural Address, April 30, 1789, *GW Papers: Pres. Ser.*, 2:175. For the frailties of republican governments, see W. Paul Adams, "Republicanism in Political Rhetoric before 1776," *Political Science Quarterly*, 35 (1970), 397–421; John R. Howe, Jr., "Republican Thought and the Political Violence of the 1790s," *American Quarterly*, 19 (1967), 147–65; and William Gribbin, "Republican Religion and American Churches in the Early National Period," *The Historian*, 35 (1972), 62–74.

3. Seymour Martin Lipset, *The First New Nation: The United States in Historical Perspective*, with a new introduction (New York, 1979), 16–20; Gouverneur Morris to Washington, Dec. 6, 1788, *GW Papers: Pres. Ser.*, 1:165–66.

4. Simon P. Newman, "Principles or Men? George Washington and the Political Culture of National Leadership, 1776–1801," *Journal of the Early Republic*, 12 (1992), 482–84; Mason L. Weems, *The Life of Washington*, ed. Marcus Cunliffe (Cambridge, Mass., 1962), 132–34.

5. Ellen G. Miles, *George and Martha Washington: Portraits from the Presidential Years* (Charlottesville, Va., 1999), 15. The social and cultural aspects of Washington's presidency is the theme of a recent excellent issue of *White House History*, 6 (1999).

6. Inducted into Masonry as a very young man in Fredericksburg, Virginia, Washington never showed any real interest in the organization, rarely attending meetings at any time in his life, although he participated as a Mason in the laying of the cornerstone of the Capitol in 1793. Some Americans viewed it as too elitist and secretive to be a

positive influence in a republic. Although he accepted the presidency of the Society of the Cincinnati when it was formed at the end of the Revolutionary War and continued to hold that office until his death, he recognized that many of his countrymen saw it as a hereditary group that might operate as a kind of military pressure group in public affairs. He was scarcely active, even though holding its highest office, and he never attended a general meeting after 1787. He favored a decentralized society and opposed its hereditary provisions. At one time he advocated the abolition of the society. Steven C. Bullock, *Revolutionary Brotherhood: Freemasonry and the Transformation of the American Social Order, 1730–1840* (Chapel Hill, N.C., 1996), 80–82, 137, 162, 165–67, 178–83, 341 n74; Minor Myers, Jr., *Liberty without Anarchy: A History of the Society of the Cincinnati* (Charlottesville, Va., 1983), 56–66, 71–73, 94–95, 96–97, 199.

7. Robert M. S. McDonald, "Thomas Jefferson and Historical Self-Construction: The Earth Belongs to the Living?" *The Historian*, 62 (1999), 290–310 and "Thomas Jefferson's Changing Reputation as Author of the Declaration of Independence: The First Fifty Years," *Journal of the Early Republic*, 19 (1999), 169–96.

8. Kenneth R. Bowling and Helen E. Veit, eds., *The Diary of William Maclay and Other Notes on Senate Debates* (Baltimore, 1988), 21.

9. Donald Jackson and Dorothy Twohig, eds., *The Diaries of George Washington*, 6 vols. (Charlottesville, Va., 1976–79), 5:474–75, 6:29, 123–32.

10. *Memoir of Colonel Benjamin Tallmadge* (1904; New York, 1968), 62; Washington to Andrew Eliot, Dec. 1, 1783, GW: *Writings*, 27:251–52; *Pennsylvania Packet*, Nov. 29, 1783. Judith Van Buskirk generously provided these citations.

11. For Washington's relationship with Smith and Washington College, see GW *Papers: Conf. Ser.*, 1:38n, 371–72. For Tench Coxe, see Jacob E. Cooke, *Tench Coxe and the Early Republic* (Chapel Hill, N.C., 1978), chaps. 1–2. Only seventeen (3.4%) appointees to the Washington and Adams administrations were identifiable loyalists. Carl E. Prince, *The Federalists and the Origins of the U.S. Civil Service* (New York, 1977), 270, 276.

12. Roberta Jacobs, "The Treaty and the Tories: The Ideological Reaction to the Return of the Loyalists" (unpub. Ph.D. diss., Cornell Uni-

versity, 1974); Higginbotham, "The American Militia," in *Reconsiderations on the Revolutionary War*, ed. Higginbotham, 83–103; Jonathan Clark, "The Problem of Allegiance in Revolutionary Poughkeepsie," in *Saints & Revolutionaries: Essays on Early American History*, eds. David D. Hall, John M. Murrin, and Thad W. Tate (New York, 1984), 285–317; Robert M. Calhoon, "The Reintegration of the Loyalists and the Disaffected," in *The American Revolution: Its Character and Its Limits*, ed. Jack P. Greene (New York, 1987), 51–74; Joseph S. Tiedemann, *Reluctant Revolutionaries: New York City and the Road to Independence, 1763–1776* (Ithaca, N.Y., 1997) and Tiedemann's articles cited in Calhoon, "Reintegration of the Loyalists," 70, 72. I have been privileged to examine some of the unpublished work in progress by Judith Van Buskirk on loyalties in and around New York City and by Lawrence E. Babits on soldiers switching sides, especially those who at one time or another were members of Banastre Tarleton's Tory Legion. One of my own graduate students discovered years ago that there was an important untold story about the shaky loyalties of many men in the Tory Legion. Michael R. Nifong, "In the Provincial Service: The British Legion in the American Revolution, 1778–1783" (unpubl. M.A. thesis, University of North Carolina at Chapel Hill, 1976).

13. John P. Kaminski, *George Clinton: Yeoman Politician of the New Republic* (Madison, Wis., 1993), 5, 188; Richard R. Beeman, *Patrick Henry: A Biography* (New York, 1974), 186–87; Stephen B. Presser, "The Verdict on Samuel Chase and His 'Apologist,'" in *Seriatim: The Supreme Court before John Marshall*, ed. Scott Douglas Gerber (New York and London, 1998), 260–91, defends a controversial jurist, who was talented and temperamental.

14. Washington to Jonathan Trumbull, Jr., July 20, 1788, *GW Papers: Conf. Ser.*, 6:389. Of course, Washington did not reconcile with all Antifederalists. The most notable exception was George Mason, his friend and political ally of over three decades. Peter R. Henriques, "An Uneven Friendship: The Relationship Between George Washington and George Mason," *Virginia Magazine of History and Biography*, 97 (1989), 185–204.

15. First Inaugural Address, [April 30, 1789], Washington to Madison, c. May 31, 1789, *GW Papers: Pres. Ser.*, 2:176, 419; Leibiger, *Founding Friendship*, 121.

16. Washington to the Governor and Council of North Carolina, June 19, 1789, Madison to Washington, Nov. 20, 1789, *GW Papers: Pres. Ser.*, 4:47–49, 309; Leibiger, *Founding Friendship*, 122.

17. Circular to the Governors of the States, Oct. 2, 1789, *GW Papers: Pres. Ser.*, 4:125–27.

18. Washington to the Hebrew Congregation in Newport, Rhode Island, Aug. 18, 1790, *GW Papers: Pres. Ser.*, 6:284–85. See generally Boller, *Washington and Religion*.

19. He made one exception, for his secretary Tobias Lear's twenty-three-old wife, Polly, who died in the 1793 yellow fever epidemic. Stephen Decatur, Jr., *Private Affairs of George Washington: From the Records and Accounts of Tobias Lear, Esquire, his Secretary* (1933; New York, 1969), 129, 181.

20. Paul Leicester Ford, *Washington and the Theater* (New York, 1899); Brown, *Theater in America*, 59, 65, 138–39, 142, 167; Hugh F. Rankin, *The Theater in Colonial America* (Chapel Hill, N.C., 1960).

21. Schutz and Adair, eds., *The Spur of Fame*, 181.

22. For Adams's views on Washington, see the excellent summary in Joseph J. Ellis, *Passionate Sage: The Character and Legacy of John Adams* (New York, 1993), 66–68 and notes. Adams listed nine characteristics of Washington in Schutz and Adair, eds., *The Spur of Fame*, 97–98, quotation on p. 98.

23. David S. Shields, *Civil Tongues and Polite Letters in British America* (Chapel Hill, N.C., 1997), 320–21. For a remarkable book still of great value after nearly a century and a half, see Rufus Wilmot Griswold, *The Republican Court: or American Society in the Days of Washington* (New York, 1855).

24. There is no indication, however, that Washington believed women should hold federal office, even at the lowest levels. When Mary Katherine Goddard was removed from her position as postmistress of Baltimore, after holding the office for fourteen years, Washington refused to intervene in her behalf, stating that the matter was in the hands of Postmaster General Samuel Osgood. The Postmaster General said only in response to Mrs. Goddard that he stood by his decision to appoint a man who could perform the duties of the office more effectively than his predecessor. *GW Papers: Pres. Ser.*, 4:426–29.

25. Abigail Adams to Mary Cranch, Aug. 9, 1789, Stewart Mitchell, ed., *New Letters of Abigail Adams* (Boston, 1947), 19; Shields, *Civil Tongues and Polite Letters*, 320–21 and conversations with the author based on his continuing work on the republican court. The concept of separate gender spheres receives strong backing in Linda K. Kerber, *Women of the Republic: Intellect and Ideology in Revolutionary America* (Chapel Hill, N.C., 1980). For criticism of the republican court, see Catherine Allgor, *Parlor Politics: In Which the Ladies of Washington Help Build a City and a Government* (Charlottesville, Va., 2000), 19–23.

26. W. W. Abbot, "George Washington, the West, and the Union," *Indiana Magazine of History*, 84 (1988), 3–14, quotation on p. 14.

27. Washington to François Jean Chastellux, Oct. 12, 1783, Washington Papers, Library of Congress, to Richard Henry Lee, Dec. 14, 1784, *GW Papers: Conf. Ser.* 2:182.

28. Washington to Jacob Read, Nov. 3, 1784, *GW Papers: Conf. Ser.*, 2:118–22, esp. 121, one of a number of letters Washington wrote that year expressing this theme. For a detailed account of the "Threat of Disunion in the West: Editorial Note," see Boyd et al., eds., *Jefferson Papers*, 19:429–518.

29. George Nicholas to James Madison, May 8, 1789, Hutchinson et al., eds., *Madison Papers*, 12:140.

30. Arthur St. Clair to Washington, Aug. 1789, *GW Papers: Pres. Ser.*, 3:580–90, quotations on p. 585.

31. Andrew R. L. Cayton, "'Separate Interests' and the Nation-State: The Washington Administration and the Origins of Regionalism in the Trans-Appalachian West," *Journal of American History*, 79 (1992), 39–67.

32. Washington to Edmund Pendleton, Jan. 22, 1795, *GW Writings*, 34:98–101. John Baker Holroyd, Baron Sheffield of Dunamore, in 1783 published *Observations on the Commerce of the American States*, which as early as 1784 was already in its sixth printing. He rejected the idea of modifying British trade restrictions on the United States and, as Washington said, predicted the dissolution of the United States. Charles R. Ritcheson, *Aftermath of the Revolution: British Policy Toward the United States, 1783–1795* (Dallas, Tex., 1971), 5–7, 33–34, and throughout.

33. Washington to Sir Edward Needham, Aug. 29, 1788, *GW Papers: Conf. Ser.*, 6:487.

34. Washington to Henry Laurens, Nov. 14, 1778, *GW Writings*, 13:254–57; Washington to Thomas Jefferson, Jan. 1, 1788, Washington to La Luzerne, Feb. 7, 1788, Washington to Jonathan Trumbull, Jr., July 20, 1788, *GW Papers: Conf. Ser.*, 6:4, 99, 389.

35. Washington to David Humphreys, July 25, 1785, *GW Papers: Conf. Ser.*, 3:148–51, quotations on pp. 148–49.

36. Washington to William Moultrie, Aug. 28, 1793, *GW Writings*, 33:73.

37. John C. Miller, *The Federalist Era, 1789–1801* (New York, 1960), 155–54; Gaillard Hunt, ed., *Division Sentiment in Congress in 1794* (Washington, D.C., 1905), 21–23.

38. Washington to Patrick Henry, Oct. 9, 1795, *GW Writings*, 34:335.

39. Newman, "Principles or Men?," 485–508.

40. Phelps, *Washington & American Constitutionalism*, 152. My essay owes much to Phelps's fine work.

41. John E. Semonche, *Keeping the Faith: A Cultural History of the U.S. Supreme Court* (Lanham, Md., and Oxford, 1998), 40–41.

42. James Iredell Grand Jury Charge, April 26, 1792, Maeva Marcus, ed., *The Documentary History of the Supreme Court of the United States, 1789–1800*, 6 vols. to date (New York, 1985–), 2:271.

43. Marshall to James Monroe, Jan. 3, 1784, Herbert Johnson et al., eds., *The Papers of John Marshall*, 10 vols. to date (Chapel Hill, N.C., 1974–), 1:113.

44. *The Papers of John Marshall*, 4:46–49, 50–51.

45. Jean Edward Smith, *John Marshall: Definer of a Nation* (New York, 1996), 328, 329. I am indebted to the author for pointing out that Robert Kenneth Faulkner's highly respected *The Jurisprudence of John Marshall* (Princeton, 1968), xviii–xix, emphasizes Marshall's *Life of Washington* as critical to understanding Marshall's jurisprudence.

46. The Marshall literature is voluminous. The chief justice acknowledged his debt to Washington in his *An Autobiographical Sketch*. Washington's influence also appears in their correspondence. R. Kent Newmyer's recent *John Marshall and the Heroic Age of the Supreme Court* (Baton Rouge, La., 2001) also emphasizes the Washington-Marshall re-

lationship. Peter R. Henriques calls my attention to a provision in Washington's will that requires adjudication of any disputes concerning its meaning by "three impartial and intelligent men," whose findings were "to be as binding on the Parties as if it had been given in the Supreme Court of the United States." Henriques, I think correctly, sees in this provision Washington's support for the Supreme Court's authority as the body or agency of final resort for questions of law and constitutionality and, implicitly at least, as a rejection of ideas about states' rights contained in the recently published Virginia and Kentucky Resolutions. W. W. Abbott et al., eds., *The Papers of George Washington: Retirement Series*, 4 vols. (Charlottesville, Va., 1998–1999), 4:492 (hereafter cited as *GW Papers: Ret. Ser.*).

CHAPTER FOUR

~

Reflections on the Unifier

Washington had worked for unity for twenty years or more when he stepped down from the presidency. At every stage, the gains were hard won—an independent nation, a national constitution, a West more securely anchored to the East, and a new federal government in operation for eight years, having weathered thus far the storms of the French Revolution and war in Europe. We could wish that the abolition of slavery had been on his agenda and that he had labored to bring it about with the tenacity that he had displayed in all his other public endeavors. It seems safe to say that he failed to take on the most intractable problem in America at least in part because the unity that he had labored so hard to bring about remained fragile. There is every reason to think that a nationwide effort by the authors of the Constitution or by his administration would have shattered the union. No proposed constitutional amendment by the Antifederalists contained such an idea. Nor did such prominent anti-slavery Federalists like John Jay or Alexander Hamilton advocate manumission by the national government. At the Constitutional Convention, Washington heard Pierce Butler of South Carolina warn that "the Southern

States" would resist efforts to take "their negroes . . . from them, which some gentlemen within or without doors, have a very good mind to do." Early in his presidency, Washington learned from his friend Dr. David Stuart that Quaker agitation over the peculiar institution led some Virginians to fear that a "Northern phalanx" now threatened the South, raising concerns about "the impractability of Union" with states of dissimilar interests.[1] In his own letters, however, Washington condemned slavery as both economically inefficient and at odds with Enlightenment ideas and the fullest implications of the American Revolution. If there is such a thing as leadership by example, then he did far more than most of the Founders who owned bondsmen, for his own slaves received their freedom as called for in his will.[2]

Long before the building of the Washington Monument, the new "Federal City," as Washington termed it, became a kind of monument to him, for it not only received his name (the City of Washington) within a year of the Residency Act of 1790 but he played an influential, behind-the-scenes role in its location on the Potomac, the midpoint between Maine and Georgia. Aware that the residence question had been the most dangerous sectional issue in the First Congress, Washington breathed easier on learning from his secretary, Tobias Lear, that the new site met with the approval of certain prominent Massachusetts Federalists, who, after earlier reservations about a southern location, now considered the anticipated national capital "the cement of union between the North and South." Congress virtually turned over to him the task of locating and planning the capital, "which he believed . . . would strengthen the Union and consequently his reputation in its history."[3]

Washington worked closely with the commissioners of the District of Columbia and approved Major Pierre Charles L'Enfant's stunning plan (over Jefferson's opposition) for a metropolis of wide boulevards and circles. He joined with the French engineer in deciding the siting of the capitol and president's house a mile apart, each taking advantage of its natural surroundings and each covered in stone (Jefferson had recommended "Roman brick"). Washington sought this expansive undertaking to be the crown jewels of the nation, although it never became the great commercial and cultural metropolis that he envisaged, nor has any created city ever attained that pre-eminence, with the exception of Peter the Great's St. Petersburg, which resulted from the monarch's use of arbitrary power and brute force. Lesser though important jewels in his constellation, had Washington prevailed with Congress, would have been the establishment of a national university and a military academy, the latter a creation of President Jefferson, who drew upon ground work laid by the first chief executive.[4] National educational institutions would enhance the process of genuine American unification. As Washington explained to Hamilton, in "the Juvenal period of life, when friendships are formed, & habits established that will stick by one; the Youth, or young men from different parts of the United States would be assembled together, & would by degrees discover that there was not that cause for those jealousies & prejudices which one part of the Union had imbibed agains[t] another part. . . . What, but the mixing of people from different parts of the United States during the War rubbed off these impressions? A Century in the ordinary intercourse, would not have accomplished what the Seven years association in Arms did."[5]

In death, Washington continued to serve as a unifier. In fact, as certain controversial domestic and foreign policy measures associated with his administration receded in time, his value to the American people increased. Unlike the ups and downs that Hamilton and Jefferson have experienced with the public and the historians, Washington has never really known a downtime. Marcus Cunliffe suggests that the Washington mythology of the nineteenth century rested on ideas and perceptions of the First of the Founders that enjoyed wide currency in his own lifetime. And a student of public rituals declares that "the forms of militia parades and ceremonies for Washington's birthday changed little between 1790 and 1860," replete with bands, orations, and dinners.[6]

All this is hardly surprising since Washington played the largest role of any individual in shaping a revolution and then a nation. He alone in American history demonstrated that a great warrior could also be a great political leader. Unlike Taylor, Grant, and Eisenhower, he proved an exception to the rule that few leaders are men for all seasons. He was the American center-piece in a centripetal Revolutionary process extending over two decades. The Revolution became, as Clifford Geertz would say, a story—fact and fiction—of a common past, an invaluable if not an essential element in holding a nation together, something, as he has noted, that Third World nations like Indonesia rarely pos-sess.[7] Of course, some parts of the American story would be sub-ject to different interpretations, such as the Constitution.

Not so Washington. His character and accomplishments gen-erated no major divisions between Democrats and Whigs or be-tween North and South. Indeed, for Edward Everett, the Massa-chusetts orator, and for Ann Pamela Cunningham, a South Carolina woman, Washington's memory and his great house served as a reminder of the soldier president's importance for all Americans as they worked to raise money and to organize women from throughout the nation to save his decaying mansion on the Potomac. The year 1856 saw the formation of the Mount Vernon Ladies Association of the Union, which purchased Mount Ver-non on the eve of the Civil War. The organization, which sur-vived the conflict, became the first historic preservation agency in the nation. Not only Mount Vernon but also Washington's personal papers, which he carefully organized and preserved, helped his countrymen to remain mindful of his accomplish-ments and his commitment to a united America. Beginning in the 1830s, several editions have appeared. What will surely be the definitive edition, *The Papers of George Washington*—thus far numbering nearly fifty volumes, including his diaries—has passed the halfway mark. The undertaking is sponsored by the University of Virginia and the Mount Vernon Ladies' Association, with generous financial assistance from other sources such as the National Endowment for the Humanities and the National Historical Publications and Records Commission.[8]

For Washington the Unifier, his letters and public messages abound with expressions such as "Union," "Nation," "National Character," and "United people"—almost always capitalized. If Washington frequently used the vocabulary of republicanism to describe the American political scene—referring to the sovereignty of the people and to values of prudence, modesty, and virtue (a "republican style of living") as essential to good citizenship and good leadership, he also tapped still another contemporary idiom of political discourse. Isaac Kramnick calls it "the state-centered language of power."[9] It permeated his "Sentiments" and his "Circular to the States," as well as countless letters to state and national dignitaries. Although Washington did not share Hamilton's monarchical leanings, the president and his secretary of the treasury shared a vocabulary of political centralization. Along with the above-mentioned words such as "Union" and "National Character," we find that "system," "security," "strength," "vigor," "energy," "public good," and "political reformation" also shaped their literary conversation.

A union without national power, in Washington's mind, amounted to little or nothing. His views on power and the ways in which it should be used for national ends are further illuminated in Edmund S. Morgan's *The Genius of George Washington*. Morgan shows that Washington's "understanding of power, both military power and political power" exceeded "that of any of his contemporaries."[10] Aware that America could not be politically transformed overnight, Washington still looked forward to the day that America could be secure at home and respected in the world. It is hardly surprising to state that Washington believed in perpetual union. He spoke publicly of his belief in "an indissoluble Union" as early as the Circular Letter in 1783, and he repeated that conviction in the Farewell Address. He had nothing to say that could be honestly claimed later by Southern nullifiers and secessionists. Politically, at least, "he was the least Virginian of the great Virginians."[11] Had his and Madison's position prevailed at the Constitutional Convention, Congress would have had a veto over all state laws.

Union is a major theme, arguably the dominate message, in the president's Farewell Address, which was printed in every major newspaper in the country. The valedictory has often been interpreted too narrowly as an assault on political party activity and a warning against entangling foreign alliances. Even those aspects of the final presidential message can be cast in the larger context of union, which is a word that appears repeatedly (and capitalized). What might be termed his obsession with national consolidation may seem overwrought to us, possibly a mantra sounded to the neglect of other matters and leading him to exaggerate, again from our view, the evils of policy divisions and parties. But we have to remember what an uphill battle union had been for Washington and how it still seemed precarious to him when he relinquished the executive office, a view shared by Federalists and Republicans alike in the 1790s, a decade that became one of the most acrimonious in our history. That tells us why he went to such length in the Farewell Address to explain what the four sections of the country—he described them as North, South, East, and West—had in common and how their very real interdependence strengthened America both at home and in the world of nations.[12]

All but forgotten owing to the justly memorable Farewell Address is yet another parting message that escaped serious attention then and now: Washington's eighth and final state of the union message to Congress. Delivered in person, unlike the Farewell Address of several months earlier, which he directed to his countrymen as a whole and not to Congress, it was the last of his many public messages, a practice that had begun with occasional circular letters to the states in the War of Independence. In this state of the union oration, he looked to the future, as he had done in the Farewell Address, but with one major difference. Whereas the former dealt with generalities and principles, the congressional speech dealt with specifics for a later day, specifics to strengthen the union and America's standing in the world of nations. Ever a realist, Washington undoubtedly knew that most of his proposals would not be adopted at the time; but he nonetheless wanted to go on record as to the direction in which the nation should move, not only after his retirement but even after his death, a plan of action for the forthcoming nineteenth century. The federal government should subsidize agriculture by gathering data and distributing funds to further new scientific discoveries. It should offer monetary inducements to free domestic manufacturers from unreliable European competition. It should implement his previous proposals for a national university and a national military academy. It should substantially expand the navy. Here again he spoke the "language of state-centered power." But he included another recommendation that showed he was no slave to the elitism of the High Federalists: he urged the lawmakers to raise the salaries of federal officeholders since public service should not be limited to the rich and wellborn, a concept antithetical to the republican "principles of our Government."[13]

What, in the final analysis, is Washington's legacy? It surely differed from that of Jefferson, with his rhetoric of individual liberty and limited government. If Jefferson heightened our sensitivity to "inalienable rights," Washington, with more than a little help, gave us a nation. If Madison's nationalism was structural and operational, creating meaningful divisions of authority between the states and the central government and between the branches of the federal government, Washington's nationalism was ideological.[14] It contained passionate visions of national supremacy, a powerful union and what he called a national character. Was all this to be at the expense of other nations and peoples? Or to frame the concern another way, did it share commonalities with crusading ideologies in modern history—with Arabs and Islam, with Spain and Catholicism, with Napoleon and revolutionary liberalism, and with Soviet and Chinese Marxian communism, or with Manifest Destiny as enunciated in America in the 1840s to justify the Mexican War and other land hunger in the nineteenth century? It seems unlikely that Washington envisioned an American domain beyond the 1783 boundaries, although both he and Jefferson spoke of an American empire, Jefferson calling it an empire of liberty. Alexander Hamilton, with ambitions toward Spain's lands to the south, dreamed unrealistically of a greater territorial realm, to say nothing of America's becoming a major player on the international scene. In contrast, Washington's goal remained to consolidate the existing American landscape.[15] Nation-building had been his mission as early as 1776, a task he was singularly equipped to pursue. It took a revolution for him to enter something more expansive than a Virginia political stage. No product of deterministic forces, he displayed, in his own unique way, the creativity of an intellectual giant. Dr. David Ramsay, a South Carolina congressman and historian, must have considered Washington as the preeminent example when he wrote that the Revolution had "not only required, but created talents," employing them "with an energy far surpassing all expectations, which could be reasonably founded on their previous acquirements."[16]

Washington's gifts surely included drive, tenacity, single-mindedness, and a vision of a kind of America, muscular and united, that few of the leading lights of his generation dared grasp. And, at least one other: he inspired enormous trust, not only from his countrymen who needed a cultural symbol but also from those who saw him up close. John Shy essayed Washington this way: "More important than professional skill or his human sensitivity is that the leader *behave* as his followers think he should—that he look, act, and sound like the leader they want." Washington could not have elicited such feeling from the men around him had he, like other great leaders, not believed "in himself and in the cause" of American union. "Belief is the real magic of leadership."[17] Whatever his abilities, he could never as a provincial have achieved renown in the old empire in the political or military realms. Nor could he have gained recognition in other areas, for he lacked endowments in the arts, literature, or science, which contemporaries on both sides of the Atlantic found in Franklin and Benjamin West. If, then, he was a product of history, he also drove history. That is to say, a country's destiny can be shaped by a great man rather than by impersonal socioeconomic forces. In this case, a man who, like the hedgehog, knew one big thing, and that was national unity. He had historical valance in abundance. Few if any political leaders in the world since then have succeeded so well or left such an extraordinary legacy as that of Washington. Even Voltaire and Hume, I suspect, would have been pleased.

Notes

1. Farrand, ed., *Records of the Federal Convention*, 1:605; David Stuart to Washington, March 15, 1790, *GW Papers: Pres. Ser.*, 5:235–38.

2. There are many references to the evils of slavery in Washington's letters, particularly after 1785. His ideas on how to eradicate the institution, gradual emancipation acts by the state legislatures, were usually confined to his correspondence. Paul F. Bowler, Jr., "Washington, the Quakers, and Slavery," *Journal of Negro History*, 46 (1961), 83–88; John E. Ferling, *The First of Men: A Life of George Washington* (Knoxville, Tenn., 1988), 475–80; Dorothy Twohig, "'That Species of Property': George

Washington's Role in the Controversy over Slavery," in *George Washington Reconsidered*, ed. Don Higginbotham (Charlottesville, Va., 2001), 114–38. See also Fritz Hirschfeld, *George Washington and Slavery: A Documentary Portrayal* (Columbia, Mo. and London, 1997).

3. Kenneth R. Bowling, *The Creation of Washington, D.C.: The Ideas and Location of the American Capital* (Fairfax, Va., 1991), chaps. 7–8, quotations on pp. 208, 225. Washington's concern over "fixing the seat of the government" is stated candidly in his letter to the Marquis de La Luzerne, Aug. 10, 1790, *GW Papers: Pres. Ser.*, 6:229.

4. Theodore J. Crackel, "The Founding of West Point: Jefferson and the Politics of Security," *Armed Forces and Society*, 7 (1981), 529–43 and *Mr. Jefferson's Army* (New York, 1987). In his will, Washington bequeathed his Potomac Company stock "towards the endowment of a University to be established within the limits of the District of Columbia, under the auspices of the General Government." *GW Papers: Ret. Ser.*, 4:483, 496.

5. Harold C. Syrett, ed., *The Papers of Alexander Hamilton*, 27 vols. (New York, 1961–1987), 20:311–12. For the reasons that the national capital never reached Washington's expectations, see C. M. Harris, "Washington's Gamble, L'Enfant's Dream: Politics, Design, and the Founding of the National Capital," *William and Mary Quarterly*, 3d ser., 56 (1999), 527–64; Stanley Elkins and Eric McKitrick, *The Age of Federalism* (New York, 1993), 184–93.

6. Weems, *Life of Washington*, ix–lxii, esp. xliii, xlv. The reference to rituals appears in Susan G. Davis, *Parades and Power: Street Theater in Nineteenth-Century Philadelphia* (Philadelphia, 1986), 59. For treatments of other Revolutionary leaders in later times, see Bernard Mayo, *Myths and Men: Patrick Henry, George Washington, Thomas Jefferson* (Athens, Ga., 1959), chap. 2; Merrill D. Peterson, *The Jeffersonian Image in the American Mind* (New York and Oxford, 1960); Robert Glenn Parkinson, "A Founder Held 'Hostage': The Image of Thomas Jefferson in the Civil Rights Movement, 1954–1968" (M.A. thesis, University of Tennessee, Knoxville, 1998); Peter Onuf, ed., *Jeffersonian Legacies* (Charlottesville, Va., 1993), esp. chaps. 6, 13, 14; William A. Bryan, *George Washington in American Literature, 1775–1865* (New York, 1952); Albanese, *Sons of the Fathers*, chap. 5; and Lawrence J. Friedman, *Inventors of the Promise Land* (New York, 1975), chap. 2.

7. Clifford Geertz, *After the Fact: Two Countries, Four Decades, One Anthropologist* (Cambridge, Mass., 1995), 27. See also Eric Hobsbawm, *The Invention of Tradition* (Cambridge, Eng., 1983).

8. John Hope Franklin, "The North, the South, and the American Revolution," *Journal of American History*, 62 (1975), 5–23; Henry Steele Commager, "The Search for a Usable Past," in Commager, *The Search for a Usable Past and Other Essays in Historiography* (New York, 1967), 13–27; Dalzell and Dalzell, *Washington's Mount Vernon*, 225–27; Dorothy Eaton, *Index to the George Washington Papers* (Washington, D.C., 1964), traces the history of the manuscripts from the family to the Library of Congress; W. W. Abbot, "An Uncommon Awareness of Self: The Papers of George Washington," *Prologue*, 29 (1989), 7–19, includes information on the current editorial project. On at least one occasion Washington endeavored to retrieve a significant document bearing on his military career. After returning to Mount Vernon in December, 1783, he wrote to the Secretary of Congress: "If my Commission [as commander in chief] is not necessary for the files of Congress I should be glad to have it deposited amongst my own Papers." Washington to Charles Thompson, Jan. 22, 1784, *GW Papers: Conf. Ser.*, 1:71. The commission was returned to him.

9. Isaac Kramnick, "The 'Great National Discussion': The Discourse of Politics in 1787," *William and Mary Quarterly*, 3d ser., 45 (1988), 23–32, esp. 24.

10. Edmund S. Morgan, *The Genius of George Washington* (Washington, D.C., 1980), 6.

11. W. W. Abbot, *The Young George Washington and His Papers* (Charlottesville, Va., 1999), 16.

12. It is hard to understand why historians have wasted so much ink over the respective contributions of Madison and Hamilton to the Farewell Address since the document, if not the actual wording, contains only ideas long held by Washington. I agree with much of Matthew Spalding and Patrick J. Garrity's stimulating study, *A Sacred Union of Citizens: George Washington's Farewell Address and the American Character* (Lantham, Md., 1996). See also Victor Hugo Paltsits, ed., *Washington's Farewell Address* (New York, 1935); Felix Gilbert, *The Beginnings of American Foreign Policy: To the Farewell Address* (New York, 1961); and Burton Ira Kaufman, ed., *Washington's Farewell Address: The View from the 20th Century* (Chicago, 1969).

13. *GW Writings*, 37:978–85; Syrett, ed., *Hamilton Papers*, 20:382–88. Joseph J. Ellis points out the differences between the Farewell Address and the neglected final state of the union message in "The Farewell: Washington's Wisdom at the End," in *George Washington Reconsidered*, ed. Higginbotham, chap. 9 and in a slightly expanded form in his Pulitzer Prize–winning *Founding Brothers: The Revolutionary Generation* (New York, 2001), chap. 4. It seems sensible to contend that Washington "employed presidential speech to control the proliferation of voices and the multiplication of interests . . . that," in his view, "threatened the nation." Sandra M. Gustafson, *Eloquence Is Power: Oratory & Performance in Early America* (Chapel Hill, N.C., 2000), 234. Washington wished to use every available means to convey his messages to the public, especially to Americans in the West, where ties to the union seemed most tenuous. Therefore, he fully supported federal legislation increasing dramatically the number of post offices and decreasing postal rates for newspapers. Richard R. John, *Spreading the News: The American Postal System from Franklin to Morris* (Cambridge, Mass., 1995), 53–60.

14. Peterson, *Jeffersonian Image*; Joyce Appleby, "Jefferson and His Complex Legacy," in *Jeffersonian Legacies*, ed. Onuf, 1–16; Carl L. Becker, "What Is Still Living in the Political Philosophy of Thomas Jefferson?" *Proceedings of the American Philosophical Society*, 87 (1944), 201–10; Lance Banning, "The Practicable Sphere of a Republic: James Madison, the Constitutional Convention, and the Emergence of Revolutionary Federalism," in *Beyond Confederation: Origins of the Constitution and American National Identity*, eds. Richard R. Beeman et al. (Chapel Hill, N.C. 1987), 162–87, "James Madison and the Nationalists, 1780–1783," *William and Mary Quarterly*, 3d ser., 40 (1983), 227–55, and *The Sacred Fire of Liberty: James Madison & the Founding of the Federal Republic* (Ithaca, N.Y. and London, 1995).

15. Marshall Smelser, "George Washington Declines El Liberator," *William and Mary Quarterly*, 3d ser., 9 (1954), 42–51; John C. Miller, *Alexander Hamilton: Portrait in Paradox* (New York, 1959), chap. 32.

16. David Ramsay, *The History of the American Revolution*, 2 vols. (Philadelphia, 1789), 2:316.

17. John Shy, "General Washington Reconsidered," in *The John Biggs Cincinnati Lectures in Military and Leadership Command*, ed. Henry S. Bausum (Lexington, Va., 1986), 51–52.

APPENDIXES

~

Selected Washington State Papers

The following documents, which are discussed in the text, cast important light on Washington's record as a nation-maker. It is arguable that he was *the* penman of the American Revolution.

∾

Sentiments on a Peace Establishment, May 1783

A Peace Establishment for the United States of America may in my opinion be classed under four different heads Vizt:

First. A regular and standing force, for Garrisoning West Point and such other Posts upon our Northern, Western, and Southern Frontiers, as shall be deemed necessary to awe the Indians, portect our Trade, prevent the encroachment of out Neighbours of Canada and the Florida's, and guard us at least from surprizes; Also for security of our Magazines.

Secondly. A well organized Militia; upon a Plan that will pervade all the States, and introduce similarity in their Establishment Manœuvres, Exercise and Arms.

Thirdly. Establishing Arsenals of all kinds of Military Stores.

Fourthly. Accademies, one or more for the Instruction of the Art Military; particularly those Branches of it which respect Engineering and Artillery, which are highly essential, and the knowledge of which, is most difficult to obtain. Also Manufactories of some kinds of Military Stores.

Upon each of these, and in the order in which they stand, I shall give my sentiments as concisely as I can, and with that freedom which the Committee have authorized.

Altho' a *large* standing Army in time of Peace hath ever been considered dangerous to the liberties of a Country, yet a few Troops, under certain circumstances, are not only safe, but indispensably necessary. Fortunately for us our relative situation requires but few. The same circumstances which so effectually retarded, and in the end conspired to defeat the attempts of Britain to subdue us, will now powerfully tend to render us secure. Our *distance* from the European States in a great degree frees us of apprehension, from their numerous regular forces and the Insults and dangers which are to be dreaded from their Ambition.

But, if our danger from those powers was more imminent, yet we are too poor to maintain a standing Army adequate to our defence, and was our Country more populous and rich, still it could not be done without great oppression of the people. Besides, as soon as we are able to raise funds more than adequate to the discharge of the Debts incurred by the Revolution, it may become a Question worthy of consideration, whether the surplus should not be applied in preparations for building and equipping a Navy, without which, in case of War we could neither protect our Commerce, nor yield that Assistance to each other, which, on such an extent of Sea-Coast, our mutual Safety would require.

Fortifications on the Sea Board may be considered in two points of view, first as part of the general defence, and next, as securities to Dock Yards, and Arsenals for Ship Building, neither of which shall I take into this plan; because the first would be difficult, if not, under our circumstances, impracticable; at any rate amazingly expensive. The other, because it is a matter out of my line, and to which I am by no means competent, as it requires a consideration of many circumstances, to which I have never paid attention.

The Troops requisite for the Post of West Point, for the Magazines, and for our Northern, Western and Southern Frontiers, ought, in my opinion, to amount to 2631 Officers of all denominations included; besides the Corps of Invalids. If this number should be thought large, I would only observe; that the British Force in Canada is now powerful, and, by report, will be increased; that the frontier is very extensive; that the Tribes of Indians within our Territory are numerous, soured and jealous; that Communications must be established with the exterior Posts; And, that it may be policy and œconomy, to appear respectable in the Eyes of the Indians, at the Commencement of our National Intercourse and Traffic with them. In a word, that it is better to reduce our force hereafter, by degrees, than to have it to increase after some unfortunate disasters may have happened to the Garrisons; discouraging to us, and an inducement to the Enemy to attempt a repetition of them.

Besides these Considerations, we are not to forget, that altho' by the Treaty, half the Waters, and the free Navigation of the Lakes appertain to us, yet, in Case of a rupture with Great Britain we should in all probability, find little benefits from the Communications with our upper Posts, by the Lakes Erie and Ontario; as it is to be presumed, that the Naval superiority which they now have on those Waters, will be maintained. It follows as a Consequence then, that we should open new or improve the present half explored Communications with Detroit and other Posts on the Lakes, by the Waters of the Susquehannah Potowmack or James River, to the Ohio, from whence, with short Portages several Communications by Water may be opened with Lake Erie. To do which, posts should be established at the most convenient places on the Ohio. This would open several doors for the supply of the Garrisons on the Lakes; and is absolutely necessary for such others as may be tho't advisable to establish upon the Mississippi.

The Ohio affording the easiest, as well as the safest Route to the Illinois settlements, and the whole Country below on the Mississippi, quite to our Southern boundary.

To protect the Peltry and Fur Trade, to keep a watch upon our Neighbours, and to prevent their encroaching upon our Territory undiscovered, are all the purposes that can be answered by an extension of our Posts, at this time, beyond Detroit, to the Northward or Westward: but, a strong Post on the Scioto, at the carrying place between it and the River Sandusky, which empties into Lake Erie, mentioned in Hutchins's Description of that Country Page 24, and more plainly pointed out by Evans's Map, is indispensably necessary for the security of the present Settlers, and such as probably, will *immediately* settle within those Limits. And by giving security to the Country and covering its Inhabitants, will enable them to furnish supplies to the Garrisons Westward and Northward of these settlements, upon moderate and easy Terms.

The 2,631 Men beforementioned, I would have considered to all Intents and Purposes as Continental Troops; looking up to Congress for their Orders, their pay, and supplies of every kind. The Infantry of which, being 1908 and, composing four Regiments may be thrown into the following disposition [see Table 1].

Not having that *particular* knowledge of the situation of the Southern and Western Boundaries of the Carolinas and Georgia, which is necessary to decide on the Posts to be established in that District, the allotment of only one Regiment thereto, may be judged inadequate; should that be the case, a greater force may be established and a sufficient allowance made them.

The above establishment differs from our present one, in the following instances Vizt: The exclusion of the light Company and reducing a sergeant and 18 Privates from each of the Battalion Companies, and giving a Chaplain to each Regiment instead of a Brigade. If it should be asked why the Reduction of non commisd. Officers and Privates is made, while the Commissioned Officers remain the same? It may be answered, that the number of Men which compose the Infantry, will be sufficient for my Calculation, and that the situation of our Frontiers renders it convenient to divide them into so many Corps as have been mentioned, for the ease and propriety of Command. I may also say, that in my Opinion, the number of our Commissioned Officers, has always been disproportionate to the Men. And that in the detached State in which these Regiments must be employed, they cannot consistently with the good of Service be reduced.

It may also be observed, that in case of War and a necessity of assembling their Regiments in the Field, nothing more will be necessary, than to recruit 18 Men to each Compy. and give the Regiment its flank Company. Or if we should have occasion to add strength to the Garrisons, or increase the number of our Posts, we may augment 900 Men including Serjeants, without requiring more than the Officers of 4 Companies, or exceeding our present Establishment. In short, it will give us a Number of Officers well skilled in the Theory and Art of War, who will be ready on any occasion, to mix and diffuse their knowledge of Discipline to other Corps, without that lapse of Time, which, without such Provision, would be necessary to bring intire new Corps acquainted with the principles of it.

Besides the 4 Regiments of Infantry, one of Artillery will be indispensably necessary. The Invalid Corps should also be retained. Motives of humanity, Policy and justice will all combine to prevent their being disbanded. The numbers of the last will, from the nature of their composition, be fluctuating and uncertain. The establishment of the former will be as follows, Vizt [see Table 2]:

To this Regiment of Artillery should be annexed 50 or 60 Artificers, of the various kinds which will be necessary, who

Table 1 Establishment and Disposition of Four Regts. of Infantry 1908 Men including Officers

Disposition	Colonel	Lt. Colonel	Major	Captains	Lieuts.	Ensigns	Chaplain	Adjutant	P Master	Qr. Master	Surgeon	Mate	Sergt. Major	Qr. Mr. Sergt.	Drum Major	Fife Major	Sergeants	Drum & Fifes	Rank & File	Total
	Officers — Commissioned						*Officers — Staff*						*Non Comd. Officers*							
Penobscot or St. Croix or both............	1	1		3	3	3						1	1	1			9	6	150	
North End of Lake Champlain..........			1	4	4	4	1	1	1	1	1				1	1	12	8	200	
Connecticut River near the 45th Degree..........				1		1											2	1	30	
Ticonderoga..........					1												1	1	20	
Establishment & Strength...	1	1	1	8	8	8	1	1	1	1	1	1	1	1	1	1	24	16	400	477
Niagara..........	1		1	3	3	3	1	1	1	1	1				1	1	9	6	150	
Oswego..........				1	1	1											2	1	30	
Fort Erie No. end of Lake Erie..																	1	1	20	
Detroit..........		1		3	3	3						1	1	1			9	6	150	
Streights between Lake Huron & Superior..........				1	1	1											3	2	50	
Establishment & Strength....	1	1	1	8	8	8	1	1	1	1	1	1	1	1	1	1	24	16	400	477

Fort Pitt..........	1		1	1	1	1	1					1	1	1	1	1	2	1	30	
Mouth of the Scioto																	1	1	20	
Portage between Scioto & Sandusky..........				3	3	3				1							9	6	150	
Mouth of Kentucky or the Rapids..........				1	1	1					1						2	1	30	
Mouth of the Ohio or near it....								1	1								1	1	20	
Height at the mouth of the River Illinois..........		1		3	3	3											9	6	50	
Establishment & Strength...	1	1	1	8	8	8	1	1	1	1	1	1	1	1	1	1	24	16	400	477
To be disposed, as those who are best acquainted with the Frontiers of the Carolinas & Georgia May direct..........	1	1	1	8	8	8	1	1	1	1	1	1	1	1	1	1	24	16	400	477
Establishment & Strength of 4 Regts..........	4	4	4	32	32	32	4	4	4	4	4	4	4	4	4	4	96	64	1600	1908

Table 2 Establishment for One Regiment of Artillery

Category		Position	Number
		Total	723
		Matrosses	390
Officers	Non Commissioned	Drums & Fifes	20
		Gunners	60
		Bombadiers	60
		Corporals	60
		Sergeants	60
		Fife Major	1
		Drum Major	1
		Qur. M. Sergeant	1
		Serjt. Major	1
	Staff	Mate	1
		Surgeon	1
		Qur. Master	1
		Pay Mr.	1
		Adjutant	1
		Chaplain	1
	Commissioned	2nd Lieutenants	30
		1st Lieutenants	10
		Captn. Lieuts.	10
		Captains	10
		Major	1
		Lieut. Colonel	1
		Colonel	1

may be distributed in equal numbers into the different Companies and being part of the Regiment, will be under the direction and Command of the Commanding Officer, to be disposed into different services as Circumstances shall require. By thus blending Artificers with Artillery, the expence of Additional Officers will be saved; and they will Answer all the purposes which are to be expected from them, as well as if formed into a distinct Corps.

The Regiment of Artillery, with the Artificers, will furnish all the Posts in which Artillery is placed, in proportionate numbers to the Strength and importance of them. The residue, with the Corps of Invalids, will furnish Guards for the Magazines, and Garrison West Point. The importance of this last mentioned Post, is so great, as justly to have been considered, the key of America; It has been so pre-eminently advantageous to the defence of the United States, and is still so necessary in that view, as well as for the preservation of the Union, that the loss of it might be productive of the most ruinous Consequences. A Naval superiority at Sea and on Lake Champlain, connected by a Chain of Posts on the Hudson River, would effect an entire separation of the States on each side, and render it difficult, if not impracticable for them to co-operate.

Altho' the total of the Troops herein enumerated does not amount to a large number, yet when we consider their detached situation, and the extent of Country they are spread over: the variety of objects that are to be attended to, and the close inspection that will be necessary to prevent abuses or to correct them before they become habitual; not less than two General Officers in my opinion will be competent to the Duties to be required of them. They will take their Instructions from the Secretary of War, or Person acting at the Head of the Military Department, who will also assign them their respective and distinct Districts. Each should twice a Year visit the

Posts of his particular District, and notice the Condition they are in, Inspect the Troops, their discipline and Police, Examine into their Wants, and see that strict justice is rendered them and to the Public, they should also direct the Colonels, at what intermediate Times they shall perform the like duties at the Posts occupied by the Detachments of their respective Regiments. The visiting General ought frequently, if not always, to be accompanied by a Skillful Engineer, who should point out such alterations and improvements as he may think necessary from time to time, for the defence of any of the Posts; which, if approved by the General, should be ordered to be carried into execution.

Each Colonel should be responsible for the Administration of his Regiment; and when present, being Commanding Officer of any Post, which is occupied by a Detachment from his Regt., he may give such directions as he may think proper, not inconsistent with the Orders of his Superior Officer, under whose general superintendence the Troops are. He will carefully exact Monthly Returns from all detachments of his Regiment; and be prepared to make a faithful report of all occurrences, when called upon by the General Officer in whose Department he may be placed and whose instructions he is at all times to receive and obey. These Returns and Reports, drawn into a General one, are to be transmitted to the Secretary at War, by the visiting General, with the detail of his own proceedings, remarks and Orders.

The three Years Men now in service will furnish the proposed Establishment, and from these, it is presumed, the Corps must in the first Instance be composed. But as the pay of an American Soldier is much greater than any other we are acquainted with; and as there can be little doubt of our being able to obtain them in time of Peace, upon as good Terms as other Nations, I would suggest the propriety of inlisting those who may come after the present three years Men, upon Terms of similarity with those of the British, or any other the most liberal Nations.

When the Soldiers for the War have frolicked a while among their friends, and find they must have recourse to hard labour for a livelyhood, I am persuaded numbers of them will reinlist upon almost any Terms. Whatever may be adopted with respect to Pay, Clothing and Emoluments, they should be clearly and unequivocally expressed and promulgated, that there may be no deception or mistake. Discontent, Desertion and frequently Mutiny, are the natural consequences of these; and it is not more difficult to know how to punish, than to prevent these inconveniences, when it known, that there has been delusion on the part of the Recruiting Officer, or a breach of Compact on the part of the public. The pay of the Battalion Officer's is full low, but those of the Chaplain, Surgeon and Mate are too high; and a proper difference should be made between the Non-Commissioned Officers (serjeants particularly) and Privates, to give them that pride and consequence which is necessary to Command.

At, or before the Time of discharging the Soldiers for the War, the Officers of the Army may signify their wishes either to retire, upon the Half pay, or to continue in the service; from among those who make the latter choice, the number wanted for a Peace Establishment may be selected; and it were to be wished, that they might be so blended together from the Several Lines, as to remove, as much as possible, all Ideas of State distinctions.

No forage should be allowed in time of Peace to Troops in Garrison, nor in any circumstances, but when actually on a March.

Soldiers should not be inlisted for *less* than three Years, to commence from the date of their attestations; and the more difference there is in the commencement of their terms of Service, the better; this Circumstance will be the means of avoiding the danger and inconvenience of entrusting any important Posts to raw Recruits unacquainted with service.

Rum should compose no part of a Soldier's Ration; but Vinegar in large quantities should be issued. Flour or Bread, and a stipulated quantity of the different kinds of fresh or Salted Meat, with Salt, when the former is Issued, is all that should be contracted for.

Vegetables they can, and ought to be compelled to raise. If spruce, or any other kind of small Beer, could be provided, it ought to be given gratis, but not made part of the Compact with them. It might be provided also, that they should receive one or two days fish in a Week, when to be had; this would be a saving to the public, (the Lakes and most of the Waters of the Ohio and Mississippi abounding with Fish) and would be no disservice to the Soldier.

A proper recruiting fund should be established; from which the Regiment may always be kept complete.

The Garrisons should be changed as often as it can be done with convenience; long continuance in the same place is injurious. Acquaintances are made, Connections formed, and habits acquired, which often prove very detrimental to the service. By this means, public duty is made to yield to interested pursuits, and real abuses are the Result. To avoid these Evils, I would propose, that there should be a change made in every Regiment once a Year, and one Regiment with another every two Years.

An Ordinance for the service of Troops in Garrison, should be annexed to our present Regulations for the order and discipline of the Army. The latter should be revised, corrected and enlarged so as to form a Basis of Discipline under all circumstances for Continental Troops, and, as far as they will apply, to the Militia also: that one uniform system may pervade all the States.

As a peace establishment may be considered as a change in, if not the Commencement of our Military system, it will be the proper time, to introduce new and beneficial regulations, and to expunge all customs, which from experience have been found unproductive of general good. Among the latter I would ask, if promotion by Seniority is not one? That it is a good general rule admits of no doubt, but that it should be an invariable one, is in my opinion wrong. It cools, if it does not destroy, the incentives to Military Pride and Heroic Actions. On the one hand, the sluggard, who keeps within the verge of his duty, has noting to fear. On the other hand, the enterprising Spirit has nothing to expect. Whereas, if promotion was the *sure* reward of Merit, *all* would contend for Rank and the service would be benefited by their Struggles for Promotion. In establishing a mode by which this is to be done, and from which nothing is to be expected, or apprehended, either from favour or prejudice, lies the difficulty. Perhaps, reserving to Congress the right inherent in Sovereignties, of making all Promotions. A Board of superior Officers, appointed to receive and examine the claims to promotions out of common course, of any Officer, whether founded on a particular merit, or extra service, and to report their opinion thereon to Congress; might prove a likely means of doing justice. It would certainly give a Spur to Emulation, without endangering the rights, or just pretentions of the Officers.

Before I close my observations under this head, of a regular force, and the Establishment of Posts, it is necessary for me to observe, that, in fixing a Post at the North End of Lake Champlain I had three things in view. The Absolute Command of the entrance into the Lake from Canada. A cover to the Settlements on the New Hampshire Grants and the prevention of any illicit intercourse thro' that Channel. But, if it is known, or should be found, that the 45th Degree crosses the Lake South of any spot which will command the entrance into it, the primary object fails; And it then becomes a question whether any place beyond Ticonderoga or Crown Point is eligible.

Altho' it may be somewhat foreign to, and yet not altogether unconnected with the present subject, I must beg leave,
from the importance of the object, as it appears to my mind,
and for the advantages which I think would result from it to
the United States, to hint, the propriety of Congress taking
some early steps, by a liberal treatment, to gain the affections
of the French settlements of Detroit, those of the Illinois and
other back Countries. Such a measure would only hold out
great encouragement to the Inhabitants already on those
lands, who will doubtless make very useful and valuable subjects of the United States; but would probably make deep and
conciliatory impressions on their friends in the British settlements, and prove a means of drawing thither great numbers of
Canadian Emigrants, who, under proper Regulations and establishments of Civil Government, would make a hardy and
industruous race of Settlers on that Frontier; and who, by
forming a barrier against the Indians, would give great security
to the Infant settlement, which, soon after the close of the
War, will probably be forming in the back Country.

I come next in the order I have prescribed myself, to treat
of the Arrangements necessary for placing the Militia of the
Continent on a respectable footing for the defence of the Empire and in speaking of this great Bulwark of our Liberties and
independence, I shall claim the indulgence of suggesting
whatever general observations may occur from experience and
reflection with the greater freedom, from a conviction of the
importance of the subject; being persuaded, that the immediate safety and future tranquility of this extensive Continent
depend in a great measure upon the peace Establishment now
in contemplation; and being convinced at the same time, that
the only probable means of preventing insult or hostility for
any length of time and from being excepted from the conse-
quent calamities of War, is to put the National Militia in such
a condition as that they may appear truly respectable in the

Eyes of our Friends and formidable to those who would other-wise become our enemies.

Were it not totally unnecessary and superfluous to adduce arguments to prove what is conceded on all hands the Policy and expediency of resting the protection of the Country on a respectable and well established Militia, we might not only shew the propriety of the measure from our peculiar local situation, but we might have recourse to the Histories of Greece and Rome in their most virtuous and Patriotic ages to demonstrate the Utility of such Establishments. Then passing by the Mercinary Armies, which have at one time or another subverted the liberties of allmost all the Countries they have been raised to defend, we might see, with admiration, the Freedom and Independence of Switzerland supported for Centuries, in the midst of powerful and jealous neighbours, by means of a hardy and well organized Militia. We might also derive useful lessons of a similar kind from other Nations of Europe, but I believe it will be found, the *People of this Continent* are too well acquainted with the Merits of the subject to require information or example. I shall therefore proceed to point out some general outlines of their duty, and conclude this head with a few particular observations on the regulations which I conceive ought to be immediately adopted by the States at the instance and recommendation of Congress.

It may be laid down as a primary position, and the basis of our system, that every Citizen who enjoys the protection of a free Government, owes not only a proportion of his property, but even of his personal services to the defence of it, and consequently that the Citizens of America (with a few legal and official exceptions) from 18 to 50 Years of Age should be borne on the Militia Rolls, provided with uniform Arms, and so far accustomed to the use of them, that the Total strength of the Country might be called forth at a Short Notice on any very interesting Emergency, for these purposes they ought to be duly organized into Commands of the same formation; (it is not of *very* great importance, whether the Regiments are large or small, provided a sameness prevails in the strength and composition of them and I do not know that a better establishment, than that under which the Continental Troops now are, can be adopted. They ought to be regularly Mustered and trained, and to have their Arms and Accoutrements inspected at certain appointed times, not less than once or twice in the course of every [year] but as it is obvious, amongst such a Multitude of People (who may indeed be useful for temporary service) there must be a great number, who from domestic Circumstances, bodily defects, natural awkwardness or disinclination, can never acquire the habits of Soldiers; but on the contrary will injure the appearance of any body of Troops to which they are attached, and as there are a sufficient proportion of able bodied young Men, between the Age of 18 and 25, who, from a natural fondness for Military parade (which passion is almost ever prevalent at that period of life) might easily be enlisted or drafted to form a Corps in every State, capable of resisting any sudden impression which might be attempted by a foreign Enemy, while the remainder of the National forces would have time to Assemble and make preparations for the Field. I would wish therefore, that the former, being considered as a *denier resort*, reserved for some great occasion, a judicious system might be adopted for forming and placing the latter on the best possible Establishment. And that which the Men of this description shall be viewed as the Van and flower of the American Forces, ever ready for Action and zealous to be employed whenever it may become necessary in the service of their Country; they should meet with such exemptions, privileges or distinctions, as might tend to keep alive a true Military pride, a nice sense of honour, and a patriotic regard for the public. Such sentiments, indeed, ought to be instilled into our Youth, with their earliest years, to be cherished and inculcated as frequently and forcibly as possible.

It is not for me to decide positively, whether it will be ultimately most interesting to the happiness and safety of the United States, to form this Class of Soldiers into a kind of Continental Militia, selecting every 10th 15th or 20th. Man from the Rolls of each State for the purpose; Organizing, Officering and Commissioning those Corps upon the same principle as is now practiced in the Continental Army. Whether it will be best to comprehend in this body, all the Man fit for service between some given Age and no others, for example between 28 and 25 or some similar description, or whether it will be preferable in every Regiment of the proposed Establishment to have one additional Company inlisted or drafted from the best Men for 3, 5, or 7 years and distinguished by the name of the additional or light Infantry Company, always to be kept complete. These Companies might then be drawn together occasionally and formed into particular Battalions or Regiments under Field Officers appointed for that Service. One or other of these plans I think will be found indispensably necessary, if we are in earnest to have an efficient force ready for Action at a moments Warning. And I cannot conceal my private sentiment, that the formation of additional, or light Companies will be most consistent with the genius of our Countrymen and perhaps in their opinion most consonant to the spirit of our Constitution.

I shall not contend for names or forms, it will be altogether essential, and it will be sufficient that perfect Uniformity should be established throughout the Continent, and pervade, as far as possible, every Corps, whether of standing Troops or Militia, and of whatever denomination they may be. To avoid the confusion of a contrary practice, and to produce the happy consequences which will attend a uniform system of Service, in case Troops from the different parts of the continent shall ever be brought to Act together again, I would beg leave to propose, that Congress should employ some able hand, to digest a Code of Military Rules and regulations, calculated immediately for the Militia and other Troops of the United States; And as it should seem the present system, by being a little simplified, altered, and improved, might be very well adopted to the purpose; I would take the liberty of recommending, that measures should be immediately taken for the accomplishment of this interesting business, and that an Inspector General should be appointed to superintend the execution of the proposed regulations in the several States.

Congress having fixed upon a proper plan to be established, having caused the regulations to be compiled, having approved, Printed and distributed them to every General Field Officer, Captain and Adjutant of Militia, will doubtless have taken care, that whenever the system shall be adopted by the States the encouragement on the one hand, and the fines and penalties on the other will occasion an universal and punctual compliance therewith.

Before I close my remarks on the establishment of our National Militia, which is to be the future guardian of those rights and that Independence, which have been maintain'd so gloriously, by the fortitude and perseverance of our Countrymen, I shall descend a little more minutely to the interior arrangements, and sum up what I have to say on this head with the following Positions.

1st. That it appears to me extremely necessary there should be an Adjutant General appointed in each State, with such Assistants as may be necessary for communicating the Orders of the Commander in Chief of the State, making the details, collecting the Returns and performing every other duty incident to that Office. A duplicate of the Annual Returns should always be lodged in the War Office by the 25th of Decr. in every year, for the information of Congress; with any other reports that may be judged expedient. The Adjutant Generals and Assistants to be considered as the deputies of the Inspector General, and to assist him in carrying the system of Discipline into effect.

2d. That every Militia Officer should make himself acquainted with the plan of Discipline, within a limited time, or forfeit his Commission, for it is in vain to expect the improvement of the Men, while the Officers remain ignorant, which many of them will do, unless Government will make and enforce such a Regulation.

3dly. That the formation of the Troops ought to be perfectly simple and entirely uniform, for example each Regiment should be composed of two Battalions, each Battalion to consist of 4 Companies and each Company as at present of 1 Captain, 1 Lieutenant, 1 Ensign, 5 Sergeants, 3 Corporals, 1 Music, 65 Privates.

Two Battalions should form a Regiment four Regts a Brigade and two Brigades a Division. This might be the general formation; but as I before observed, I conceive it will be eligible to select from the district forming a Regiment, the flower of the young Men to compose an additional or light Company to every Regiment, for the purposes before specified, which undoubtedly ought to be the case unless something like a Continental Militia shall be instituted. To each Division two Troops of Cavalry and two Companies of Artillery might also be annexed, but no Independent or Volunteer Companies foreign to the Establishment should be tolerated.

4thly. It is also indispensable that such a proportion of the Militia (under whatever discription they are comprehended) as are always to be held in readiness for service, nearly in the same manner the Minute Men formerly were, should be excercised at least from 12 to 25 days in a year, part of the time in Company, part in Battalion and part in Brigade, in the latter case, by forming a Camp, their Discipline would be greatly promoted, and their Ideas raised, as near as possible, to real service; Twenty five days might be divided thus, ten days for training in squads, half Companies and Companies, ten in Battalion and five in Brigade.

5thly. While in the field or on actual duty, there should not only be a Compensation for the time thus spent, but a full allowance of Provisions Straw, Camp Equipage &c; it s also of so great consequence that there should be, a perfect similarity in the Arms and Accoutrements, that they ought to be furnished, in the first instance by the public, if they cannot be obtained in any other way, some kind of Regimentals or Uniform Clothing (however cheap or course they may be) are also highly requisite and should be provided for such occasions. Nor is it unimportant that every Article should be stamped with the appearance of regularity; and especially that all the Articles of public property should be numbered, marked or branded with the name of the Regiment or Corps that they may be properly accounted for.

6thly. In addition to the Continental Arsenals, which will be treated of under the next head. Every State ought to Establish Magazines of its own, containing Arms, Accoutrements, Ammunitions, all kinds of Camp Equipage and Warlike Stores, and from which the Militia or any part of them should be supplied whenever they are call'd into the Field.

7thly. It is likewise much to be wished, that it might be made agreeable to Officers who have served in the Army, to accept Commands in the Militia; that they might be appointed to them so far as can be done without creating uneasiness and jealousy, and that the principle Characters in the Community would give a countenance to Military improvements, by being present at public reviews and Exhibitions, and by bringing into estimation amongst their fellow Citizens, those who appear fond of cultivating Military knowledge and who excel in the Exercise of Arms. By giving such a tone to our Establishment; by making it universally reputable to bear Arms and disgraceful to decline having a share in the performance of Military duties; in fine, by keeping up in Peace "a well regulated, and disciplined Militia," we shall take the fairest and best method to preserve, for a long time to come, the happiness, dignity and Independence of our Country.

With regard to the third Head in Contemplation, to wit. the "Establishment of Arsenals of all kinds of Military Stores." I will only observe, that having some time since seen a plan of The Secretary of War, which went fully into the discussion of this branch of Arrangement, and appeared (as well as I can, at this time recollect) to be in general perfectly well founded, little more need be said on the subject, especially as I have been given to understand the plan has been lately considerably improved and laid before Congress for their approbation; and indeed there is only one or two points in which I could wish to suggest any Alteration.

According to my recollection, five grand Magazines are proposed by the Secretary at War, one of which to be fixed at West Point. Now, as West Point is considered not only by our selves, but by all who have the least knowledge of the Country, as a post of the greatest importance, as it may in time of Peace, from its situation on the Water be somewhat obnoxious to surprise or *Coup de Main* and as it would doubtless be a first object with any Nation which might commence a War against the United States, to seize that Post and occupy or destroy the Stores, it appears to me, that we ought particularly to guard against such an event, so far as may be practicable, and to remove some part of the Allurements to enterprise, by establishing the grand Arsenals in the Interior part of the Country, leaving only to West Point an adequate supply for its defence in almost any extremity.[1]

I take the liberty also to submit to the consideration of the Committee, whether, instead of five great Arsenals, it would not be less expensive and equally convenient and advantageous to fix three general Deposits, one for the Southern, one for the Middle and one for the Eastern States, including New York, in each of which there might be deposited, Arms,

Ammunition, Field Artillery, and Camp Equipage for thirty thousand Men, Also one hundred heavy Cannon and Mortars, and all the Apparatus of a Seige, with a sufficiency of Ammunition.

Under the fourth General Division of the subject, it was proposed to consider the Establishment of Military Academies and Manufacturies, as the means of preserving that knowledge and being possessed of those Warlike Stores, which are essential to the support of the Sovereignty and Independence of the United States. But as the Baron Steuben has thrown together his Ideas very largely on these Articles, which he had communicated to me previous to their being sent to the secretary at War, and which being now lodged at the War Office, I imagine have also been submitted to the inspection of the Committee, I shall therefore have the less occasion for entering into the detail, and may, without impropriety, be the more concise in my own observations.

That an Institution calculated to keep alive and diffuse the knowledge of the Military Art would be highly expedient, and that some kinds of Military Manufactories and Elaboratories may and ought to be established, will not admit a doubt; but how far we are able at this time to go into great and expensive Arrangements and whether the greater part of the Military Apparatus and Stores which will be wanted can be imported or Manufactured, in the cheapest and best manner: I leave those to whom the observations are to be submitted, to determine, as being more competent, to the decision than I can pretend to be. I must however mention some things, which I think cannot be dispensed with under the present or any other circumstances; Until a more perfect system of Education can be adopted, I would propose that Provision should be made at some Post or Posts where the principle Engineers and Artillerists shall be stationed, for instructing a certain number of young Gentlemen in the Theory of the Art of War, particularly in all those branches of service which belong to the Artillery and Engineering Departments. Which, from the affinity they bear to each other, and the advantages which I think would result from the measure, I would have blended together; And as this species of knowledge will render them much more accomplished and capable of performing the duties of Officers, even in the Infantry or any other Corps whatsoever, I conceive that appointments to vacancies in the Established Regiments, ought to be made from the candidates who shall have completed their course of Military Studies and Exercises. As it does in an essential manner qualify them for the duties of Garrisons, which will be the principal, if not only service in which our Troops can be employed in time of Peace and besides the Regiments of Infantry by this means will become in a time a nursery from whence a number of Officers for Artillery and Engineering may be drawn on any great or sudden occasion.

Of so great importance is it to preserve the knowledge which has been acquired thro' the various Stages of a long and arduous service, that I cannot conclude without repeating the necessity of the proposed Institution, unless we intend to let the Science become extinct, and to depend entirely upon the Foreigners for their friendly aid, if ever we should again be involved in Hostility. For it must be understood, that a Corps of able Engineers and expert Artillerists cannot be raised in a day, nor made such by any exertions, in the same time, which it would take to form an excellent body of Infantry from a well regulated Militia.

And as to Manufactories and Elaboratories it is my opinion that if we should not be able to go largely into the business at present, we should nevertheless have a reference to such establishments hereafter, and in the means time that we ought to have such works carried on, wherever our principal Arsenals may be fixed, as will not only be sufficient to repair and keep in good order the Arms, Artillery, Stores & of the Post, but shall also extend to Founderies and some other essential matters.

Thus I have given my sentiments without reserve on the four different heads into which the subject seemed naturally to divide itself, as amply as my numerous avocations and various duties would permit. Happy shall I be, if any thing I have suggested may be found of use in forming an Establishment which will maintain the lasting Peace, Happiness and Independence of the United States.

Reprinted from GW: *Writings*, 26: 374–98.

Note

1. West Point had been designated as the main depository of all the military stores of the Army after the signing of the preliminary treaty of peace.

∾

Circular to State Governments, June 1783

Head Quarters, Newburgh, June 8, 1783

Sir: The great object for which I had the honor to hold an appointment in the Service of my Country, being accomplished, I am now preparing to resign it into the hands of Congress, and to return to that domestic retirement, which, it is well known, I left with the greatest reluctance, a Retirement, for which I have never ceased to sigh through a long and painful absence, and in which (remote from the noise and trouble of the World) I meditate to pass the remainder of life in a state of undisturbed repose; But before I carry this resolution into effect, I think it a duty incumbent on me, to make this my last official communication, to congratulate you on the glorious events which Heaven has been pleased to produce in our favor, to offer my sentiments respecting some important subjects, which appear to me, to be intimately connected with the tranquility of the United States, to take my leave of your Excellency as a public Character, and to give my final blessing to that Country, in whose service I have spent the prime of my life, for whose sake I have consumed so many anxious days and watchfull nights, and whose happiness being extremely dear to me, will always constitute no inconsiderable part of my own.

Impressed with the liveliest sensibility on this pleasing occasion, I will claim the indulgence of dilating the more copiously on the subjects of our mutual felicitation. When we consider the magnitude of the prize we contended for, the doubtful nature of the contest, and the favorable manner in which it has terminated, we shall find the greatest possible reason for gratitude and rejoicing; this is a theme that will afford infinite delight to every benevolent and liberal mind, whether the event in contemplation, be considered as the source of present enjoyment or the parent of future happiness; and we shall have equal occasion to felicitate ourselves on the lot which Providence has assigned to us, whether we view it in a natural, a political or moral point of light.

The Citizens of America, placed in the most enviable condition, as the sole Lords and Proprietors of a vast Tract of Continent, comprehending all the various soils and climates of the World, and abounding with all the necessaries and conveniencies of life, are now by the late satisfactory pacification, acknowledged to be possessed of absolute freedom and Independency; They are, from this period, to be considered as the Actors on a most conspicuous Theatre, which seems to be peculiarly designated by Providence for the display of human greatness and felicity; Here, they are not only surrounded with every thing which can contribute to the completion of private and domestic enjoyment, but Heaven has crowned all its blessings, by giving a fairer opportunity for political happiness, than any other Nation has ever been favored with. Nothing can illustrate these observations more forcibly, than a recollection of the happy conjuncture of times and circumstances, under which our Republic assumed its rank among the Nations; The foundation of our Empire was not laid in the gloomy age of

Ignorance and Superstition, but at an Epocha when the rights of mankind were better understood and more clearly defined, than at any former period, the researches of the human mind, after social happiness, have been carried to a great extent, the Treasures of knowledge, acquired by the labours of Philosophers, Sages and Legislatures, through a long succession of years, are laid open for our use, and their collected wisdom may be happily applied in the Establishment of our forms of Government; the free cultivation of Letters, the unbounded extension of Commerce, the progressive refinement of Manners, the growing liberality of sentiment, and above all, the pure and benign light of Revelation, have had a meliorating influence on mankind and increased the blessings of Society. At this auspicious period, the United States came into existence as a Nation, and if their Citizens should not be completely free and happy, the fault will be intirely their own.

Such is our situation, and such are our prospects: but notwithstanding happiness is ours, if we have a disposition to seize the occasion and make it our own; yet, it appears to me there is an option still left to the United States of America, that it is in their choice, and depends upon their conduct, whether they will be respectable and prosperous, or contemptable and miserable as a Nation; This is the time of their political probation, this is the moment when the eyes of the whole World are turned upon them, this is the moment to establish or ruin their national Character forever, this is the favorable moment to give such a tone to our Federal Government, as will enable it to answer the ends of its institution, or this may be the ill-fated moment for relaxing the powers of the Union, annihilating the cement of the Confederation, and exposing us to become the sport of European politics, which may play one State against another to prevent their growing importance, and to serve their own interested purposes. For, according to the system of Policy the States shall adopt at this moment, they will stand or fall, and by their confirmation or lapse, it is yet to be decided, whether the Revolution must ultimately be considered as a blessing or a curse: a blessing or a curse, not to the present age alone, for with our fate will the destiny of unborn Millions be involved.

With this conviction of the importance of the present Crisis, silence in me would be a crime; I will therefore speak to your Excellency, the language of freedom and of sincerity, without disguise; I am aware, however, that those who differ from me in political sentiment, may perhaps remark, I am stepping out of the proper line of my duty, and they may possibly ascribe to arrogance or ostentation, what I know is alone the result of the purest intention, but the rectitude of my own heart, which disdains such unworthy motives, the part I have hitherto acted in life, the determination I have formed, of not taking any share in public business hereafter, the ardent desire I feel, and shall continue to manifest, of quietly enjoying in private life, after all the toils of War, the benefits of a wise and liberal Government, will, I flatter myself, sooner or later convince my Countrymen, that I could have no sinister views in delivering with so little reserve, the opinions contained in this Address.

There are four things, which I humbly conceive, are essential to the well being, I may even venture to say, to the existence of the United States as an Independent Power:

First. An indissoluble Union of the States under one Federal Head.

Secondly. A sacred regard to Public Justice.

Thirdly. The adoption of a proper Peace Establishment, and

Fourthly. The prevalence of that pacific and friendly Disposition, among the People of the United States, which will induce them to forget their local prejudices and policies, to make those mutual concessions which are requisite to the general prosperity, and in some instances, to sacrifice their individual advantages to the interest of the Community.

These are the Pillars on which the glorious Fabrick of our Independency and National Character must be supported; Liberty is the Basis, and whoever would dare to sap the foundation, or overturn the Structure, under whatever specious pretexts he may attempt it, will merit the bitterest execration, and the severest punishment which can be inflicted by his injured Country.

On the three first Articles I will make a few observations, leaving the last to the good sense and serious consideration of those immediately concerned.

Under the first head, altho' it may not be necessary or proper for me in this place to enter into a particular disquisition of the principles of the Union, and to take up the great question which has been frequently agitated, whether it be expedient and requisite for the States to delegate a larger proportion of Power to Congress, or not, Yet it will be a part of my duty, and that of every true Patriot, to assert without reserve, and to insist upon the following positions, That unless the States will suffer Congress to exercise those prerogatives, they are undoubtedly invested with by the Constitution, every thing must very rapidly tend to Anarchy and confusion, That it is indispensable to the happiness of the individual States, that there should be lodged somewhere, a Supreme Power to regulate and govern the general concerns of the Confederated Republic, without which the Union cannot be of long duration. That there must be a faithfull and pointed compliance on the part of every State, with the late proposals and demands of Congress, or the most fatal consequences will ensue, That whatever measures have a tendency to dissolve the Union, or contribute to violate or lessen the Sovereign Authority, ought to be considered as hostile to the Liberty and Independency of America, and the Authors of them treated accordingly, and lastly, that unless we can be enabled by the concurrence of the States, to participate of the fruits of the Revolution, and enjoy the essential benefits of Civil Society, under a form of Government so free and uncorrupted, so happily guarded against the danger of oppression, as has been devised and adopted by the Articles of Confederation, it will be a subject of regret, that so much blood and treasure have been lavished for no purpose, that so many sufferings have been encountered without a compensation, and that so many sacrifices have been made in vain. Many other considerations might here be adduced to prove, that without an entire conformity to the Spirit of the Union, we cannot exist as an Independent Power; it will be sufficient for my purpose to mention but one or two which seem to me of the greatest importance. It is only in our united Character as an Empire, that our Independence is acknowledged, that our power can be regarded, or our Credit supported among Foreign Nations. The Treaties of the European Powers with the United States of America, will have no validity on a dissolution of the Union. We shall be left nearly in a state of Nature, or we may find by our own unhappy experience, that there is a natural and necessary progression, from the extreme of anarchy to the extreme of Tyranny; and that arbitrary power is most easily established on the ruins of Liberty abused to licentiousness.

As to the second Article, which respects the performance of Public Justice, Congress have, in their late Address to the United States, almost exhausted the subject, they have explained their Ideas so fully, and have enforced the obligations the States are under, to render compleat justice to all the Public Creditors, with so much dignity and energy, that in my opinion, no real friend to the honor and Independency of America, can hesitate a single moment respecting the propriety of complying with the just and honorable measures proposed; if their Arguments do not produce conviction, I know of nothing that will have greater influence; especially when we recollect that the System referred to, being the result of the collected Wisdom of the Continent, must be esteemed, if not perfect, certainly the least objectionable of any that could be devised; and that if it shall not be carried into immediate execution, a National Bankruptcy, with all its deplorable consequences will take place, before any different Plan can possibly be proposed and adopted; So pressing are the present circumstances! And such is the alternative now offered to the States!

The ability of the Country to discharge the debts which have been incurred in its defence, is not to be doubted, an inclination, I flatter myself, will not be wanting, the path of our duty is plain before us, honesty will be found on every experiment, to be the best and only true policy, let us then as a Nation be just, let us fulfil the public Contracts, which Congress had undoubtedly a right to make for the purpose of carrying on the War, with the same good faith we suppose ourselves bound to perform our private engagements; in the mean time, let an attention to the chearfull performance of their proper business, as Individuals, and as members of Society, be earnestly inclucated on the Citizens of America, that will they strengthen the hands of Government, and be happy under its protection: every one will reap the fruit of his labours, every one will enjoy his own acquisitions without molestation and without danger.

In this state of absolute freedom and perfect security, who will grudge to yield a very little of his property to support the common interest of Society, and insure the protection of Government? Who does not remember, the frequent declarations, at the commencement of the War, that we should be completely satisfied, if at the expence of one half, we could defend the remainder of our possessions? Where is the Man to be found, who wishes to remain indebted, for the defence of his own person and property, to the exertions, the bravery, and the blood of others, without making one generous effort to repay the debt of honor and gratitude? In what part of the

Continent shall we find any Man, or body of Men, who would not blush to stand up and propose measures, purposely calculated to rob the Soldier of his Stipend, and the Public Creditor of his due? And were it possible that such a flagrant instance of Injustice could ever happen, would it not excite the general indignation, and tend to bring down, upon the Authors of such measures, the aggravated vengeance of Heaven? If after all, a spirit of disunion or a temper of obstinancy and perverseness, should manifest itself in any of the States, if such an ungracious disposition should attempt to frustrate all the happy effects that might be expected to flow from the Union, if there should be a refusal to comply with the requisitions for Funds to discharge the annual interest of the public debts, and if that refusal should revive again all those jealousies and produce all those evils, which are now happily removed, Congress, who have in all their Transaction shewn a great degree of magnanimity and justice, will stand justified in the sight of God and Man, and the State alone which puts itself in opposition to the aggregate Wisdom of the Continent, and follows such mistaken and pernicious Councils, will be responsible for all the consequences.

For my own part, conscious of having acted while a Servant of the Public, in the manner I conceived best suited to promote the real interests of my Country; having in consequence of my fixed belief in some measure pledged myself to the Army, that their Country would finally do them compleat and ample Justice; and not wishing to conceal any instance of my official conduct from the eyes of the World, I have thought proper to transmit to your Excellency the inclosed collection of Papers, relative to the half pay and commutation granted by Congress to the Officers of the Army; From these communications, my decided sentiment will be clearly comprehended, together with the conclusive reasons which induced me, at an early period, to recommend the adoption of the measure, in the most earnest and serious manner. As the proceedings of Congress, the Army, and myself are open to all, and contain in my opinion, sufficient information to remove the prejudices and errors which may have been entertained by any; I think it unnecessary to say any thing more, than just to observe, that the Resolutions of Congress, now alluded to, are undoubtedly as absolutely binding upon the United States, as the most solemn Acts of Confederation or Legislation. As to the Idea, which I am informed has in some instances prevailed, that the half pay and commutation are to be regarded merely in the odious light of a Pension, it ought to be exploded forever; that Provision, should be viewed as it really was, a reasonable compensation offered by Congress, at a time when they had nothing else to give, to the Officers of the Army, for services then to be performed. It was the only means to prevent a total dereliction of the Service, It was a part of their hire, I may be allowed to say, it was the price of their blood and of your Independency, it is therefore more than a common debt, it is a debt of honour, it can never be considered as a Pension or gratuity, nor be cancelled until it is fairly discharged.

With regard to a distinction between Officers and Soldiers, it is sufficient that the uniform experience of every Nation of the World, combined with our own, proves the utility and propriety of the discrimination. Rewards in proportion to the aids the public derives from them, are unquestionably due to all its Servants; In some Lines, the Soldiers have perhaps generally had as ample a compensation for their Services, by the large Bounties which have been paid to them, as their Officers will receive in the proposed Commutation, in others, if besides the donation of Lands, the payment of Arrearages of Cloathing and Wages (in which Articles all the component parts of the Army must be put upon the same footing) we take into the estimate, the Bounties many of the Soldiers have received and the gratuity of one Year's full pay, which is promised to all, possibly their situation (every circumstance being duly considered) will not be deemed less eligible than that of the Officers. Should a farther reward, however, be judged equitable, I will venture to assert, no one will enjoy greater satisfaction than myself, on seeing an exemption from Taxes for a limited time, (which has been petitioned for in some instances) or any other adequate immunity or compensation, granted to the brave defenders of their Country's Cause; but neither the adoption or rejection of this proposition will in any manner affect, much less militate against, the Act of Congress, by which they have offered five years full pay, in lieu of the half pay for life, which had been before promised to the Officers of the Army.

Before I conclude the subject of public justice, I cannot omit to mention the obligations this Country is under, to that meritorious Class of veteran Non-commissioned Officers and Privates, who have been discharged for inability, in consequence of the Resolution of Congress of the 23rd of April 1782, on an annual pension for life, their peculiar sufferings, their singular merits and claims to that provision need only be known, to interest all the feelings of humanity in their behalf: nothing but a punctual payment of their annual allowance can rescue them from the most complicated misery, and nothing could be a more melancholy and distressing sight, than to behold those who have shed their blood or lost their limbs in the service of their Country, without a shelter, without a friend, and without the means of obtaining any of the necessaries or comforts of Life; compelled to beg their daily bread from door to door! Suffer me to recommend those of this discription, belonging to your State, to the warmest patronage of your Excellency and your Legislature.

It is necessary to say but a few words on the third topic which was proposed, and which regards particularly the defence of the Republic, As there can be little doubt but Congress will recommend a proper Peace Establishment for the

United States, in which a due attention will be paid to the importance of placing the Militia of the Union upon a regular and respectable footing; If this should be the case, I would beg leave to urge the great advantage of it in the strongest terms. The Militia of this Country must be considered as the Palladium of our security, and the first effectual resort in case of hostility; It is essential therefore, that the same system should pervade the whole; that the formation and discipline of the Militia of the Continent should be absolutely uniform, and that the same species of Arms, Accoutrements and Military Apparatus, should be introduced in every part of the United States; No one, who has not learned it from experience, can conceive the difficulty, expence, and confusion which result from a contrary system, or the vague Arrangements which have hitherto prevailed.

If in treating of political points, a greater latitude than usual has been taken in the course of this Address, the importance of the Crisis, and the magnitude of the objects in discussion, must be my apology: It is, however, neither my wish or expectation, that the preceding observations should claim any regard, except so far as they shall appear to be dictated by a good intention, consonant to the immutable rules of Justice; calculated to produce a liberal system of policy, and founded on whatever experience may have been acquired by a long and close attention to public business. Here I might speak with the more confidence from my actual observations, and, if it would not swell this Letter (already too prolix) beyond the bounds I had prescribed myself: I could demonstrate to every mind open to conviction, that in less time and with much less expence than has been incurred, the War might have been brought to the same happy conclusion, if the resources of the Continent could have been properly drawn forth, that the distresses and disappointments which have very often occurred, have in too many instances, resulted more from a want of energy, in the

Continental Government, than a deficiency of means in the particular States. That the inefficiency of measures, arising from the want of an adequate authority in the Supreme Power, from a partial compliance with the Requisitions of Congress in some States, and from a failure of punctuality in others, while it tended to damp the zeal of those which were more willing to exert themselves; served also to accumulate the expences of the War, and to frustrate the best concerted Plans, and that the discouragement occasioned by the complicated difficulties and embarrassments, in which our affairs were, by this means involved, would have long ago produced the dissolution of any Army, less patient, less virtuous and less persevering, that that which I have had the honor to command. But while I mention these things, which are notorious facts, as the defects of our Federal Constitution, particularly in the prosecution of a War, I beg it may be understood, that as I have ever taken a pleasure in gratefully acknowledging the assistance and support I have derived from every Class of Citizens, so shall I always be happy to do justice to the unparalleled exertion of the individual States, on many interesting occasions.

I have thus freely disclosed what I wished to make known, before I surrendered up my Public trust to those who committed it to me, the task is now accomplished, I now bid adieu to your Excellency as the Chief Magistrate of your State, at the same time I bid a last farewell to the cares of Office, and all the imployments of public life.

It remains then to be my final and only request, that your Excellency will communicate these sentiments to your Legislature at their next meeting, and that they may be considered as the Legacy of One, who has ardently wished, on all occasions, to be useful to his Country, and who, even in the shade of Retirement, will not fail to implore the divine benediction upon it.

I now make it my earnest prayer, that God would have you, and the State over which you preside, in his holy protection, that he would incline the hearts of the Citizens to cultivate a spirit of subordination and obedience to Government, to entertain a brotherly affection and love for one another, for their fellow Citizens of the United States at large, and particularly for their brethren who have served in the Field, and finally, that he would most graciously be pleased to dispose us all, to do Justice, to love mercy, and to demean ourselves with that Charity, humility and pacific temper of mind, which were the Characteristicks of the Divine Author of our blessed Religion, and without an humble imitation of whose example in these things, we can never hope to be a happy Nation.

Reprinted from GW: *Writings*, 26: 483–96.

~

To the President of the Confederation Congress, September 17, 1787

In the Convention, September 17, 1787

SIR, WE have now the honor to submit to the consideration of the United States in Congress assembled, that Constitution which has appeared to us the most advisable.

The friends of our country have long seen and desired, that the power of making war, peace and treaties, that of levying money and regulating commerce, and the correspondent executive and judicial authorities should be fully and effectually vested in the general government of the Union: but the impropriety of delegating such extensive trust to one body of men is evident—Hence results the necessity of a different organization.

It is obviously impracticable in the fœderal government of these States; to secure all rights of independent sovereignty to each, and yet provide for the interest and safety of all—Individuals entering into society, must give up a share of liberty to preserve the rest. The magnitude of the sacrifice must depend as well on situation and circumstance, as on the object to be obtained. It is at all times difficult to draw with precision the line between those rights which must be surrendered, and those which may be reserved; and on the present occasion this difficulty was encreased by a difference among the several States as to their situation, extent, habits, and particular interests.

In all our deliberations on this subject we kept steadily in our view, that which appears to us the greatest interest of every true American, the consolidation of our Union, in which is involved our prosperity, felicity, safety, perhaps our national existence. This important consideration, seriously and deeply impressed on our minds, led each State in the Convention to be less rigid on points of inferior magnitude, than might have been otherwise expected; and thus the Constitution, which we now present, is the result of a spirit of amity, and of that mutual deference and concession which the peculiarity of our political situation rendered indispensible.

That it will meet the full and entire approbation of every State is not perhaps to be expected; but each will doubtless consider, that had her interests been alone consulted, the consequences might have been particularly disagreeable or injurious to others; that it is liable to as few exceptions as could reasonably have been expected, we hope and believe; that it may promote the lasting welfare of that country so dear to us all, and secure her freedom and happiness, is our most ardent wish.

With great respect, WE have the honor to be SIR, Your Excellency's most Obedient and humble servants.

> George Washington, President.
> By unanimous Order of the
> Convention

Reprinted from *Documentary History Ratification*, 1: 305–6.

❧

First Inaugural Address, April 30, 1789

Fellow Citizens of the Senate and of the House of Representatives:

Among the vicissitudes incident to life, no event could have filled me with greater anxieties than that of which the notification was transmitted by your order, and received on the fourteenth day of the present month. On the one hand, I was summoned by my Country, whose voice I can never hear but with veneration and love, from a retreat which I had chosen with the fondest predilection, and, in my flattering hopes, with an immutable decision, as the asylum of my declining years: a retreat which was rendered every day more necessary as well as more dear to me, by the addition of habit to inclination, and of frequent interruptions in my health to the gradual waste committed on it by time. On the other hand, the magnitude and difficulty of the trust to which the voice of my Country called me, being sufficient to awaken in the wisest and most experienced of her citizens, a distrustful scrutiny into his qualifications, could not but overwhelm with despondence, one, who, inheriting inferior endowments from nature and unpractised in the duties of civil administration, ought to be peculiarly conscious of his own deficiencies. In this conflict of emotions, all I dare aver, is, that it has been my faithful study to collect my duty from a just appreciation of every circumstance, by which it might be affected. All I dare hope, is, that, if in executing this task I have been too much swayed by a grateful remembrance of former instances, or by an affectionate sensibility to this transcendent proof, of the confidence of my fellow-citizens; and have thence too little consulted my incapacity as well as disinclination for the weighty and untried cares before me; my *error* will be palliated by the motives which misled me, and its consequences be judged by my Country, with some share of the partiality in which they originated.

Such being the impressions under which I have, in obedience to the public summons, repaired to the present station; it would be peculiarly improper to omit in this first official Act, my fervent supplications to that Almighty Being who rules over the Universe, who presides in the Councils of Nations, and who providential aids can supply every human defect, that his benediction may consecrate to the liberties and happiness of the People of the United States, a Government instituted by themselves for these essential purposes: and may enable every instrument employed in its administration, to execute with success, the functions allotted to his charge. In tendering this homage to the Great Author of every public and private good, I assure myself that it expresses your sentiments not less than my own; nor those of my fellow-citizens at large, less than either: No People can be bound to acknowledge and adore the invisible hand, which conducts the Affairs of men more than the People of the United States. Every step, by which they have advanced to the character of an independent nation, seems to have been distinguished by some token of providential agency. And in the important revolution just accomplished in the system of their United Government, the tranquil deliberations, and voluntary consent of so many distinct communities, from which the event has resulted, cannot be compared with the means by which most Governments have been established, without some return of pious gratitude along with an humble anticipation of the future blessings which the past crisis, have forced themselves too strongly on my mind to be suppressed. You will join me I trust in thinking, that there are none under the influence of which, the proceedings of a new and free Government can more auspiciously commence.

By the article establishing the Executive Department, it is made the duty of the President "to recommend to your consideration, such measures as he shall judge necessary and expedient." The circumstances under which I now meet you, will acquit me from entering into that subject, farther than to refer to the Great Constitutional Charter under which you are assembled; and which, in defining your powers, designates the objects to which your attention is to be given. It will be more consistent with those circumstances, and far more congenial with the feelings which actuate me, to substitute, in place of a recommendation of particular measures, the tribute that is due to the talents, the rectitude, and the patriotism which adorn the characters selected to devise and adopt them. In these honorable qualification, I behold the surest pledges, that as on one side, no local prejudices, or attachments; no separate views, nor party animosities, will misdirect the comprehensive and equal eye which ought to watch over this great Assemblage of communities and interests: so, on another, that the foundations of our national policy, will be laid in the pure and immutable principles of private morality; and the pre-eminence of free Government, be exemplified by all the attributes which can win the affections of its Citizens, and command the respect of the world. I dwell on this prospect with every satisfaction which an ardent love for my Country can inspire: since there is no truth more thoroughly established, than that there exists in the œconomy and course of nature, an indissoluble union between virtue and happiness, between duty and advantage, between the genuine maxims of an honest and magnanimous policy, and the solid rewards of public prosperity and felicity: Since we ought to be no less persuaded that the propitious smiles of Heaven, can never be expected on a nation that disregards the eternal rules of order and right, which Heaven itself has ordained: And since the preservation of the sacred fire of liberty, and the destiny of the Republican model of Government, are justly considered as *deeply*, perhaps as *finally* staked, on the experiment entrusted to the hands of the American people.

Besides the ordinary objects submitted to your care, it will remain with your judgment to decide, how far an exercise of the occasional power delegated by the Fifth article of the Constitution is rendered expedient at the present juncture by the nature of objections which have been urged against the System, or by the degree of inquietude which has given birth to them. Instead of undertaking particular recommendations on this subject, in which I could be guided by no lights derived from official opportunities, I shall again give way to my entire confidence in your discernment and pursuit of the public good: For I assure myself that whilst you carefully avoid every alteration which might endanger the benefits of an United and effective Government, or which ought to await the future lessons of experience; a reverence for the characteristic rights of freemen, and a regard for the public harmony, will sufficiently influence your deliberations on the question how far the former can be more impregnably fortified, or the latter be safely and advantageously promoted.

To the preceding observations I have one to add, which will be most properly addressed to the House of Representatives. It concerns myself; and will therefore be as brief as possible. When I was first honoured with a call into the service of my Country, then on the eve of an arduous struggle for its liberties, the light in which I contemplated my duty required that I should renounce every pecuniary compensation. From this resolution I have in no instance departed—And being still under the impressions which produced it, I must decline as inapplicable to myself, any share in the personal emoluments, which may be indispensably included in a permanent provision for the Executive Department; and must accordingly pray that the pecuniary estimates for the Station in which I am placed, may, during my continuance in it, be limited to such actual expenditures as the public good may be thought to require.

Having thus imparted to you my sentiments, as they have been awakened by the occasion which brings us together, I shall take my present leave; but not without resorting once more to the benign Parent of the human race, in humble supplication that since he has been pleased to favour the American people, with opportunities for deliberating in perfect tranquility, and dispositions for deciding with unparellelled unanimity on the form of Government, for the security of their Union, and the advancement of their happiness; so this divine blessing may be equally *conspicuous* in the enlarged views—the temperate consultations, and the wise measures on which the success of this Government must depend.

April 30, 1789

Reprinted from *GW Papers: Pres. Ser.*, 2: 173–77.

~

Farewell Address, September 19, 1796

United States, September 19, 1796

Friends, and Fellow-Citizens: The period for a new election of a Citizen, to Administer the Executive government of the United States, being not far distant, and the time actually arrived, when your thoughts must be employed in designating the person, who is to be cloathed with that important trust, it appears to me proper, especially as it may conduce to a more distinct expression of the public voice, that I should now apprise you of the resolution I have formed, to decline being considered among the number of those, out of whom a choice is to be made.

I beg you, at the same time, to do me the justice to be assured, that this resolution has not been taken, without a strict regard to all the considerations appertaining to the relation, which binds a dutiful citizen to his country, and that, in with drawing the tender of service which silence in my situation might imply, I am influenced by no diminution of zeal for your future interest, no deficiency of grateful respect for your past kindness; but am supported by a full conviction that the step is compatible with both.

The acceptance of, and continuance hitherto in, the office to which your Suffrages have twice called me, have been a uniform sacrifice of inclination to the opinion of duty, and to a deference for what appeared to be your desire. I constantly hoped, that it would have been much earlier in my power, consistently with motives, which I was not at liberty to disregard, to return to that retirement, from which I had been reluctantly drawn. The strength of my inclination to do this, previous to the last Election, had even led to the preparation of an address to declare it to you; but mature reflection on the then perplexed and critical posture of our Affairs with foreign Nations, and the unanimous advice of persons entitled to my confidence, impelled me to abandon the idea.

I rejoice, that the state of your concerns, external as well as internal, no longer renders the pursuit of inclination incompatible with the sentiment of duty, or propriety; and am persuaded whatever partiality may be retained for my services, that in the present circumstances of our country, you will not disapprove my determination to retire.

The impressions, with which I first undertook the arduous trust, were explained on the proper occasion. In the discharge of this trust, I will only say, that I have, with good intentions, contributed towards the Organization and Administration of the government, the best exertions of which a very fallible judgment was capable. Not unconscious, in the outset, of the inferiority of my qualifications, experience in my own eyes, perhaps still more in the eyes of others, has strengthened the motives to diffidence of myself; and every day the encreasing weight of years admonishes me more and more, that the shade of retirement is as necessary to me as it will be welcome. Satisfied that if any circumstances have given peculiar value to my services, they were temporary, I have the consolation to believe, that while choice and prudence invite me to quit the political scene, patriotism does not forbid it.

In looking forward to the moment, which is intended to terminate the career of my public life, my feelings do not permit me to suspend the deep acknowledgment of that debt of gratitude which I owe to my beloved country, for the many honors it has conferred upon me; still more for the stedfast confidence with which it has supported me; and for the opportunities I have thence enjoyed of manifesting my inviolable attachment, by services faithful and persevering, though in usefulness unequal to my zeal. If benefits have resulted to our country from these services, let it always be remembered to your praise, and as an instructive example in our annals, that, under circumstances in which the Passions agitated in every direction were liable to mislead, amidst appearances sometimes dubious, viscissitudes of fortune often discouraging, in situations in which not unfrequently want of Success has countenanced the spirit of criticism, the constancy of your support was the essential prop of the efforts, and a guarantee of the plans by which they were effected. Profoundly penetrated with this idea, I shall carry it with me to my grave, as a strong incitement to unceasing vows that Heaven may continue to you the choicest tokens of its beneficence; that your Union and brotherly affection may be perpetual; that the free constitution, which is the work of your hands, may be sacredly maintained; that its Administration in every department may be stamped with wisdom and Virtue; that, in fine, the happiness of the people of these States, under the auspices of liberty, may be made complete, by so careful a preservation and so prudent a use of this blessing as will acquire to them the glory of recommending it to the applause, the affection, and adoption of every nation which is yet a stranger to it.

Here, perhaps, I ought to stop. But a solicitude for your welfare, which cannot end but with my life, and the apprehension of danger, natural to that solicitude, urge me on an occasion like the present, to offer to your solemn contemplation, and to recommend to your frequent review, some sentiments; which are the result of much reflection, of no inconsiderable observation, and which appear to me all important to the permanency of your felicity as a People. These will be offered to you with the more freedom, as you can only see in them the disinterested warnings of a parting friend, who can possibly have no personal motive to biass his counsel. Nor can I forget, as an encouragement to it, your endulgent reception of my sentiments on a former and not dissimilar occasion.

Interwoven as is the lover of liberty with every ligament of your hearts, no recommendation of mine is necessary to fortify or confirm the attachment.

The Unity of Government which constitutes you one people is also now dear to you. It is justly so; for it is a main Pillar in the Edifice of your real independence, the support of your tranquility at home; your peace abroad; of your safety; of your prosperity; of that very Liberty which you so highly prize. But as it is easy to foresee, that from different causes and from different quarters, much pains will be taken, many artifices employed, to weaken in your minds the conviction of this truth; as this is the point in your political fortress against which the batteries of internal and external enemies will be most constantly and actively (though often covertly and insidiously) directed, it is of infinite moment, that you should properly estimate the immense value of your national Union to your collective and individual happiness; that you should cherish a cordial, habitual and immoveable attachment to it; accustoming yourselves to think and speak of it as of the Palladium of your political safety and prosperity; watching for its preservation with jealous anxiety; discountenancing whatever may suggest even a suspicion that it can in any event be abandoned, and indignantly frowning upon the first dawning of every attempt to alienate any portion of our Country from the rest, or to enfeeble the sacred ties which now link together the various parts.

For this you have every inducement of sympathy and interest. Citizens by birth or choice, of a common country, that country has a right to concentrate your affections. The name of AMERI-CAN, which belongs to you, in your national capacity, must always exalt the just pride of Patriotism, more than any appellation derived from local discriminations. With slight shades of difference, you have the same Religion, Manners, Habits and political Principles. You have in a common cause fought and triumphed together. The independence and liberty you possess are the work of joint councils, and joint efforts; of common dangers, sufferings and successes.

But these considerations, however powerfully they address themselves to your sensibility are greatly outweighed by those which apply more immediately to your Interest. Here every portion of our country finds the most commanding motives for carefully guarding and preserving the Union of the whole.

The *North*, in an unrestrained intercourse with the *South*, protected by the equal Laws of a common government, finds in the productions of the latter, great additional resources of Maratime and commercial enterprise and precious materials of manufacturing industry. The *South* in the same Intercourse, benefitting by the Agency of the *North*, sees its agriculture grow and its commerce expand. Turning partly into its own channels the seamen of the *North*, it finds its particular navigation envigorated; and while it contributes, in different ways, to nourish and increase the general mass of the National navigation, it looks forward to the protection of a Maratime strength, to which itself is unequally adapted. The *East*, in a like intercourse with the *West*, already finds, and in the progressive improvement of interior communications, by land and water, will more and more find a valuable vent for the commodities which it brings from abroad, or manufactures at home. The *West* derives from the *East* supplies requisite to its growth and comfort, and what is perhaps of still greater consequence, it must of necessity owe the *secure* enjoyment of indispensable *outlets* for its own productions to the weight, influence, and the future Maritime strength of the Atlantic side of the

Union, directed by an indissoluble community of Interest as *one Nation*. Any other tenure by which the *West* can hold this essential advantage, whether derived from its own separate strength, or from an apostate and unnatural connection with any foreign Power, must be intrinsically precarious.

While then every part of our country thus feels an immediate and particular Interest in Union, all the parts combined cannot fail to find in the united mass of means and efforts greater strength, grater resource, proportionably greater security from external danger, a less frequent interruption of their Peace by foreign Nations; and, what is of inestimable value! They must derive from Union an exemption from those broils and Wars between themselves, which so frequently afflict neighbouring countries, not tied together by the same government; which their own rivalships alone would be sufficient to produce, but which opposite foreign alliances, attachments and intriegues would stimulate and imbitter. Hence likewise they will avoid the necessity of those overgrown Military establishments, which under any form of Government are inauspicious to liberty, and which are to be regarded as particularly hostile to Republican Liberty: In this sense it is, that your Union ought to be considered as a main prop of your liberty, and that the love of the one ought to endear to you the preservation of the other.

These considerations speak a persuasive language to every reflecting and virtuous mind, and exhibit the continuance of the UNION as a primary object of Patriotic desire. Is there a doubt, whether a common government can embrace so large a sphere? Let experience solve it. To listen to mere speculation in such a case were criminal. We are authorized to hope that a proper organization of the whole, with the auxiliary agency of governments for the respective Sub divisions, will afford a happy issue to the experiment. 'Tis well worth a fair and full experiment With such powerful and obvious motives to Union, affecting all parts of our country, while experience shall not have demonstrated its impracticability, there will always be reason, to distrust the patriotism of those, who in any quarter may endeavor to weaken its bands.

In contemplating the causes wch. May disturb our Union, it occurs as matter of serious concern, that any ground should have been furnished for characterizing parties by *Geographical* discriminations: *Northern* and *Southern; Atlantic* and *Western;* whence designing men may endeavour to excite a belief that there is a real difference of local interests and views. One of the expedients of Party to acquire influence, within particular districts, is to misrepresent the opinions and aims of other Districts. You cannot shield yourselves too much against the jealousies and heart burnings which spring from these misrepresentations. They tend to render Alien to each other those who ought to be bound together by fraternal affection. The Inhabitants of our Western country have lately had a useful lesson on this head. They have seen, in the Negociation by the Executive, and in the unanimous ratification by the Senate, of the Treaty with Spain, and in the universal satisfaction at that event, throughout the United States, a decisive proof how unfounded were the suspicions propagated among them of a policy in the General Government and in the Atlantic states unfriendly to their Interests in regard to the MISSISSIPPI. They have been witnesses to the formation of two Treaties, that with G: Britain and that with Spain, which secure to them every thing they could desire, in respect to our Foreign relations, towards confirming their prosperity. Will it not be their wisdom to rely for the preservation of these advantages on the UNION by wch. they were procured? Will they not henceforth be deaf to those advisers, if such there are, who would sever them from their Brethren and connect them with Aliens?

To the efficacy and permanency of Your Union, a Government for the whole is indispensable. No Alliances however strict between the parts can be an adequate substitute. They must inevitably experience the infractions and interruptions which all

Alliances in all times have experienced. Sensible of this momentous truth, you have improved upon your first essay, by the adoption of a Constitution of Government, better calculated than your former for an intimate Union, and for the efficacious management of your common concerns. This government, the off-spring of our own choice uninfluenced and unawed, adopted upon full investigation and mature deliberation, completely free in its principles, in the distribution of its powers, uniting security with energy, and containing within itself a provision for its own amendment, has a just claim to your confidence and your support. Respect for its authority, compliance with its Laws, acquiescence in its measures, are duties enjoined by the fundamental maxims of true Liberty. The basis of our political systems is the right of the people to make and to alter their Constitutions of Government. But the Constitution which at any times exists, 'till changed by an explicit and authentic act of the whole People, is sacredly obligatory upon all. The very idea of the power and the right of the People to establish Government presupposes the duty of every Individual to obey the established Government.

All obstructions to the execution of the Laws, all combinations and Associations, under whatever plausible character, with the real design to direct, controul counteract, or awe the regular deliberation and action of the Constituted authorities are distructive of this fundamental principle and of fatal tendency. They serve to organize faction, to give it an artificial and extraordinary force; to put in the place of the delegated will of the Nation, the will of a party; often a small but artful and enterprizing minority of the Community; and, according to the alternate triumphs of different parties, to make the public administration the Mirror of the ill concerted and incongruous projects of faction, rather than the organ of consistent and wholesome plans digest by common councils and modified by mutual interests. However combinations or Associations of the above description may now and then answer popular ends, they are likely, in the course of time and things, to become potent engines, by which cunning, ambitious and unprincipled men will be enabled to subvert the Power of the People, and to usurp for themselves the reins of Government; destroying afterwards the very engines which have lifted them to unjust dominion.

Towards the preservation of your Government and the permanency of your present happy state, it is requisite, not only that you steadily discountenance irregular oppositions to its acknowledged authority, but also that you resist with care the spirit of innovation upon its principles however specious the pretexts one method of assault may be to effect, in the forms of the Constitution, alterations which will impair the energy of the system, and thus to undermine what cannot be directly overthrown. In all the changes to which you may be invited, remember that time and habit are a least as necessary to fix the true character of Governments, as of other human institutions; that experience is the surest standard, by which to test the real tendency of the existing Constitution of a country; that facility in changes upon the credit of mere hypotheses and opinion exposes to perpetual change, from the endless variety of hypotheses and opinion: and remember, especially, that for the efficient management of your common interests, in a country so extensive as ours, a Government of as much vigour as is consistent with the perfect security of Liberty is indispensable. Liberty itself will find in such a Government, with powers properly distributed and adjusted, its surest Guardian. It is indeed little else than a name, where the Government is too feeble to withstand the enterprises of faction, to confine each member of the Society within the limits prescribed by the laws and to maintain all in the secure and tranquil enjoyment of the rights of person and property.

I have already intimated to you the danger of Parties in the State, with particular reference to the founding of them on Geographical discriminations. Let me now take a more comprehensive view, and warn you in the most solemn manner against the baneful effects of the Spirit of Party, generally.

This spirit, unfortunately, is inseperable from our nature, having its root in the strongest passions of the human Mind. It exists under different shapes in all Governments, more or less stifled, controuled, or repressed; but, in those of the popular form it is seen in its greatest rankness and is truly their worst enemy.

The alternate domination of one faction over another, sharpened by the spirit of revenge natural to party dissention, which in different ages and countries has perpetrated the most horrid enormities, is itself a frightful despotism. But this leads at length to a more formal and permanent despotism. The disorders and miseries, which result, gradually incline the minds of men to seek security and repose in the absolute power of an Individual: and sooner or later the chief of some prevailing faction more able or more fortunate than his competitors, turns this disposition to the purposes of his own elevation, on the ruins of Public Liberty.

Without looking forward to an extremity of this kind (which nevertheless ought not to be entirely out of sight) the common and continual mischiefs of the spirit of Party are sufficient to make it the interest and the duty of a wise People to discourage and restrain it.

It serves always to distract the Public Councils and enfeeble the Public Administration. It agitates the Community with ill founded jealousies and false alarms, kindles the animosity of one part against another, foments occasionally riot and insurrection. It opens the door to foreign influence and corruption, which find a facilitated access to the government itself through the channels of party passions. Thus the policy and the will of one country, are subjected to the policy and will of another.

There is an opinion that parties in free countries are useful checks upon the Administration of the Government and serve to keep alive the spirit of Liberty. This within certain limits is probably true, and in Governments of a Monarchical cast Patriotism may look with endulgence, if not with favour, upon the spirit of party. But in those of the popular character, in Governments purely elective, it is a spirit not to be encouraged. From their natural tendency, it is certain there will always be enough of that spirit for every salutary purpose. And there being constant danger of excess, the effort ought to be, by force of public opinion, to mitigate and assuage it. A fire not to be quenched; it demands a uniform vigilance to prevent its bursting into a flame, lest instead of warming it should consume.

It is important, likewise, that the habits of thinking in a free Country should inspire caution in those entrusted with its administration, to confine themselves within their respective Constitutional spheres; avoiding in the exercise of the Powers of one department to encroach upon another. The spirit of encroachment tends to consolidate the powers of all the departments in one, and thus to create whatever the form of government, a real despotism. A just estimate of that love of power, and proneness to abuse it, which predominates in the human heart is sufficient to satisfy us of the truth of this position. The necessity of reciprocal checks in the exercise of political power; by dividing and distributing it into different depositories, and constituting each the Guardian of the Public Weal against invasions by the others, has been evinced by experiments ancient and modern; some of them in our country and under our own eyes. To preserve them must be as necessary as to institute them. If in the opinion of the People, the distribution or modification of the Constitutional powers be in any particular wrong, let it be corrected by an amendment in the way which the Constitution designates. But let there be no change by usurpation; for though this, in one instance, may be the instrument of good, it is the customary weapon by which free governments are destroyed. The precedent must always greatly overbalance in permanent evil any partial or transient benefit which the use can at any time yield.

Of all the dispositions and habits which lead to political prosperity, Religion and morality are indispensable supports. In vain would that man claim the tribute of Patriotism, who should labour to subvert these great Pillars of human happiness, these firmest props of the duties of Men and citizens. The mere Politician, equally with the pious man ought to respect and to cherish them. A volume could not trace all their connections with private and public felicity. Let it simply be asked where is the security for property, for reputation, for life, if the sense of religious obligation *desert* the oaths, which are the instruments of investigation in Courts of Justice? And let us with caution indulge the supposition, that morality can be maintained with religion. Whatever may be conceded to the influence of refined education on minds of peculiar structure, reason and experience both forbid us to expect that National morality can prevail in exclusion of religious principle.

'Tis substantially true, that virtue or morality is a necessary spring of popular government. The rule indeed extends with more or less force to every species of free Government. Who that is a sincere friend to it, can look with indifference upon attempts to shake the foundation of the fabric.

Promote then as an object of primary importance, Institutions for the general diffusion of knowledge. In proportion as the structure of a government gives force to public opinion, it is essential that public opinion should be enlightened.

As a very important source of strength and security, cherish public credit. One method of preserving it is to use it as sparingly as possible: avoiding occasions of expence by cultivating peace, but remembering also that timely disbursements to prepare for danger frequently prevent much greater disbursements to repel it; avoiding likewise the accumulation of debt, not only by shunning occasions of expence, but by vigorous exertions in time of Peace to discharge the Debts which unavoidable wars may have occasioned, not ungenerously throwing upon poster-

ity the burthen which we ourselves ought to bear. The execution of these maxims belongs to your Representatives, but it is
necessary that public opinion should cooperate. To facilitate to
them the performance of their duty, it is essential that you
should practically bear in mind, that towards the payment of
debts there must be Revenue; that to have Revenue there must
be taxes; that taxes can be devised which are not more or less
inconvenient and unpleasant; that the intrinsic embarrassment
inseperable from the selection of the proper objects (which is
always a choice of difficulties) ought to be a decisive motive for
a candid construction of the Conduct of the Government in
making it, and for a spirit of acquiescence in the measure for obtaining Revenue which the public exigencies may at any time
dictate.

Observe good faith and justice towds. all Nations. Cultivate
peace and harmony with all. Religion and morality enjoin this
conduct; and can it be that good policy does not equally enjoin
it? It will be worthy of a free, enlightened, and, at no distant period, a great Nation, to give to mankind the magnanimous and
too novel example of a People always guided by an exalted justice
and benevolence. Who can doubt that in the course of time and
things the fruits of such a plan would richly repay any temporary
advantages wch. might be lost by a steady adherence to it? Can it
be, that Providence has not connected the permanent felicity of
a Nation with its virtue? The experiment, at least, is recommended by every sentiment which ennobles human Nature.
Alas! Is it rendered impossible by its vices?

In the execution of such a plan nothing is more essential than
that permanent, inveterate antipathies against particular Nations
and passionate attachments for others should be excluded; and that
in place of them just and amicable feelings towards all should be
cultivated. The Nation, which indulges towards another an habitual hatred, or an habitual fondness, is in some degree a slave. It is a
slave to its animosity or to its affection, either of which is sufficient

to lead it astray from its duty and its interest. Antipathy in one Nation against another, disposes each more readily to offer insult and injury, to lay hold of slight causes of umbrage, and to be haughty and intractable, when accidental or trifling occasions of dispute occur. Hence frequent collisions, obstinate envenomed and bloody contests. The Nation, prompted by ill will and resentment sometimes impels to War the Government, contrary to the best calculations of policy. The Government sometimes participates in the national propensity, and adopts through passion what reason would reject; at other times, it makes the animosity of the Nation subservient to projects of hostility instigated by pride, ambition and other sinister and pernicious motives. The peace often, sometimes perhaps the Liberty, of Nations has been the victim.

So likewise, a passionate attachment of one Nation for another produces a variety of evils. Sympathy for the favourite nation, facilitating the illusion of an imaginary common interest, in cases where no real common interest exists, and infusing into one the enmities of the other, betrays the former into a participation in the quarrels and Wars of the latter, without adequate inducement or justification: It leads also to concessions to the favourite Nation of priviledges denied to others, which is apt doubly to injure the Nation making the concessions; by unnecessarily parting with what ought to have been retained; and by exciting jealousy, ill will, and a disposition to retaliate, in the parties from whom eql. priviledges are withheld: And it gives to ambitious, corrupted, or deluded citizens (who devote themselves to the favourite Nation) facility to betray, or sacrifice the interests of their own country, without odium, sometimes even with popularity; gilding with the appearances of a virtuous sense of obligation a commendable deference for public opinion, or a laudable zeal for public good, the base or foolish compliances of ambition corruption or infatuation.

As avenues to foreign influence in innumberable ways, such attachments are particularly alarming to the truly enlightened and independent Patriot. How many opportunities do they afford to tamper with domestic factions, to practice the arts of se-duction, to mislead public opinion, to influence or awe the pub-lic Councils! Such an attachment of a small or weak, towards a great and powerful Nation, dooms the former to be the satellite of the latter.

Against the insidious wiles of foreign influence, (I conjure you to believe me fellow citizens) the jealousy of a free people ought to be *constantly* awake; since history and experience prove that foreign influence is one of the most baneful foes of Repub-lican Government. But that jealousy to be useful must be im-partial; else it becomes the instrument of the very influence to be avoided, instead of a defence against it. Excessive partiality for one foreign nation and excessive dislike of another, cause those whom they actuate to see danger only on one side, and serve to veil and even second the arts of influence on the other. Real Patriots, who may resist the intriegues of the favourite, are liable to become suspected and odious; while its tools and dupes usurp the applause and confidence of the people, to surrender their interests.

The Great rule of conduct for us, in regard to foreign Nations is in extending our commercial relations to have with them as lit-tle *political* connection as possible. So far as we have already formed engagements let them be fulfilled, with perfect good faith. Here let us stop.

Europe has a set of primary interests, which to us have none, or a very remote relation. Hence she must be engaged in frequent controversies, the causes of which are essentially foreign to our concerns. Hence therefore it must be unwise in us to implicate ourselves, by artificial ties, in the ordinary vicissitudes of her pol-itics, or the ordinary combinations and collisions of her friend-ships, or enmities:

Our detached and distant situation invites and enables us to pursue a different course. If we remain one People, under an effi-cient government, the period is not far off, when we may defy material injury from external annoyance; when we may take such an attitude as will cause the neutrality we may at any time resolve upon to be scrupulously respected; when belligerent nations, under the impossibility of making acquisitions upon us, will not lightly hazard the giving us provocation; when we may choose peace or war, as our interest guided by our justice shall Counsel.

Why forego the advantages of so peculiar a situation? Why quit our own to stand upon foreign ground? Why, by interweaving our destiny with that of any part of Europe, entangle our peace and prosperity in the toils of European Ambition, Rivalship, Interest, Humour or Caprice?

'Tis our true policy to steer clear of permanent Alliances, with any portion of the foreign world. So far, I mean, as we are now at liberty to do it, for let me not be understood as capable of patronising infidility to existing engagements (I hold the maxim no less applicable to public than to private affairs, that honesty is always the best policy). I repeat it therefore, let those engagements be observed in their genuine sense. But in my opinion, it is unnecessary and would be unwise to extend them.

Taking care always to keep ourselves, by suitable establishments, on a respectably defensive posture, we may safely trust to temporary alliances for extraordinary emergencies.

Harmony, liberal intercourse with all Nations, are recommended by policy, humanity and interest. But even our Commercial policy should hold an equal impartial hand: neither seeking nor granting exclusive favours or preferences; consulting the natural course of things; diffusing and deversifying by gentle means the streams of Commerce, but forcing nothing; establishing with Powers so disposed; in order to give to trade a stable course, to define the rights of our Merchants, and to enable the Government to support them; conventional rules of intercourse, the best that present circumstances and mutual opinion will permit, but temporary, and liable to be from time to time abandoned or varied, as experience and circumstances shall dictate; constantly keeping in view, that 'tis folly in one Nation to look for disinterested favors from another; that it must pay with a portion of its Independence for whatever it may accept under that character; that by such acceptance, it may place itself in the condition of having given equivalents for nominal favours and yet of being reproached with ingratitude for not giving more. There can be no greater error than to expect, or calculate upon real favours from Nation to Nation. 'Tis an illusion which experience must cure, which a just pride ought to discard.

In offering to you, my Countrymen these counsels of an old and affectionate friend, I dare not hope they will make the strong and lasting impression, I could wish; that they will control the usual current of the passions, or prevent our Nation from running the course which has hitherto marked the Destiny of Nations: But if I may even flatter myself, that they may be productive of some partial benefit, some occasional good; that they may now and then recur to moderate the fury of party spirit, to warn against the mischiefs of foreign Intriegue, to guard against the Impostures of pretended patriotism; this hope will be a full recompence for the solicitude for your welfare, by which they have been dictated.

How far in the discharge of my Official duties, I have been guided by the principles which have been delineated, the public Records and other evidences of my conduct must Witness to You and to the world. To myself, the assurance of my own conscience is, that I have at least believed myself to be guided by them.

In relation to the still subsisting War in Europe, my Proclamation of the 22d. of April 1793 is the index to my Plan. Sanctioned by your approving voice and by that of Your Representatives in both Houses of Congress, the spirit of that measure has continually governed me; uninfluenced by any attempts to deter or divert me from it.

After deliberate examination with the aid of the best lights I could obtain I was well satisfied that our Country, under all the circumstances of the case, had a right to take, and was bound in duty and interest, to take a Neutral position. Having taken it, I determined, as far as should depend upon me, to maintain it, with moderation, perseverence and firmness.

The considerations, which respect the right to hold this conduct, it is not necessary on this occasion to detail. I will only observe, that according to my understanding of the matter, that right, so far from being denied by any of the Belligerent Powers has been virtually admitted by all.

The duty of holding a Neutral conduct may be inferred, without any thing more, from the obligation which justice and humanity impose on every Nation, in cases in which it is free to act, to maintain inviolate the relations of Peace and amity towards other Nations.

The inducements of interest for observing that conduct will best be referred to your own reflections and experience. With me, a predominant motive has been to endeavour to gain time to our country to settle and mature its yet recent institutions, and to progress without interruption, to that degree of strength and consistency, which is necessary to give it, humanly speaking, the command of its own fortunes.

Though in reviewing the incidents of my Administration, I am unconscious of intentional error, I am nevertheless too sensible of my defects not to think it probable that I may have committed many errors. Whatever they may be I fervently beseech the Almighty to avert or mitigate the evils to which they may tend. I shall also carry with me the hope that my Country will never cease to view them with indulgence; and that after forty five years of my life dedicated to its Service, with an upright zeal, the faults of incompetent abilities will be consigned to oblivion, as myself must soon be to the Mansions of rest.

Relying on its kindness in this as in other things, and actuated by that fervent love towards it, which is so natural to a Man, who views in it the native soil of himself and his progenitors for several Generations; I anticipate with pleasing expectation that retreat, in which I promise myself to realize, without alloy, the sweet enjoyment of partaking, in the midst of my fellow Citizens, the benign influence of good Laws under a free Government, the ever favourite object of my heart, and the happy reward, as I trust, of our mutual cares, labours and dangers.

Reprinted from *GW: Writings*, 35: 214–38.

~

Eighth Annual Message to Congress, December 7, 1796

Fellow Citizens of the Senate and House of Representatives: In recurring to the internal situation of our Country, since I had last the pleasure to Address you, I find ample reason for a renewed expression of that gratitude to the ruler of the Universe, which a continued series of prosperity has so often and so justly called forth.

The Acts of the last Session, which required special arrangements, have been as far as circumstances would admit, carried into operation.

Measures calculated to insure a continuance of the friendship of the Indians, and to preserve peace along the extent of our interior frontier, have been digested and adopted. In the framing of these, care has been taken to guard on the one hand, our advanced Settlements from the predatory incursions of those unruly Individuals, who cannot be restrained by their Tribes; and on the other hand, to protect the rights secured to the Indians by Treaty; to draw them nearer to the civilized state; and inspire them with correct conceptions of the Power, as well as justice of the Government.

The meeting of the deputies from the Creek Nation at Colerain, in the State of Georgia, which had for a principal object the purchase of a parcel of their land, by that State, broke up without its being accomplished; the Nation having, previous to their departure, instructed them against making any Sale; the occasion however has been improved, to confirm by a new Treaty with the Creeks, their pre-existing engagements with the United States; and to obtain their consent, to the establishment of Trading Houses and Military Posts within their boundary; by means of which, their friendship, and the general peace, may be more effectually secured.

The period during the late Session, at which the appropriation was passed, for carrying into effect the Treaty of Amity, Commerce, and Navigation, between the United States and his Britannic Majesty, necessarily procrastinated the reception of the Posts stipulated to be delivered, beyond the date assigned for that event. As soon however as the Governor General of Canada could be addressed with propriety on the subject, arrangements were cordially and promptly concluded for their evacuation; and the United States took possession of the principal of them, comprehending Oswego, Niagara, Detroit, Michelimackina, and Fort Miami; where, such repairs, and additions have been ordered to be made, as appeared indispensible.

The Commissioners appointed on the part of the United States and of Great Britain, to determine which is the river S. Croix, mentioned in the Treaty of peace of 1783, agreed in the choice of Egbert Benson Esqr. Of New York, for the third Commissioner. The whole met at St. Andrews, in Passamaquoddy Bay, in the beginning of October; and directed surveys to be made of the Rivers in dispute; but deeming it impracticable to have these Surveys completed before the next Year, they adjourned, to meet at Boston in August 1797, for the final decision of the question.

Other Commissioners appointed on the part of the United States, agreeably to the seventh Article of the Treaty with

Great Britain, relative to captures and condemnations of Vessels and other property, met the Commissioners of his Britannic Majesty in London, in August last, when John Trumbull, Esqr. was chosen by lot, for the fifth Commissioner. In October following the Board were to proceed to business. As yet there has been no communication of Commissioners on the part of Great Britain, to unite with those who have been appointed on the part of the United States, for carrying into effect the sixth Article of the Treaty.

The Treaty with Spain, required, that the Commissioners for running the boundary line between the territory of the United States, and his Catholic Majesty's Provinces of East and West Florida, should meet at the Natchez, before the expiration of six Months after the exchange of the ratifications, which was effected at Aranjuez on the 25th. day of April; and the troops of his Catholic Majesty occupying any Posts within the limits of the United States, were within the same period to be withdrawn. The Commissioner of the United States therefore, commenced his journey for the Natchez in September; and troops were ordered to occupy the Posts from which the Spanish Garrisons should be withdrawn. Information has been recently received, of the appointment of a Commissioner on the part of his Catholic Majesty for running the boundary line, but none of any appointment, for the adjustment of the claims of our Citizens, whose Vessels were captured by the Armed Vessels of Spain.

In pursuance of the Act of Congress, passed in the last Session, for the protection and relief of American Seamen, Agents were appointed, one to reside in Great Britain, and the other in the West Indies. The effects of the Agency in the West Indies, are not yet fully ascertained; but those which have been communicated afford grounds to believe, the measure will be beneficial. The Agent destined to reside in Great Britain, declining to accept the appointment, the business has consequently devolved on the Minister of the United States in London; and will command his attention, until a new Agent shall be appointed.

After many delays and disappointments, arising out of the European War, the final arrangements for fulfilling the engagements made to the Dey and Regency of Algiers, will, in all present appearance, be crowned with success: but under great, tho' inevitable disadvantages, in the pecuniary transactions, occasioned by that War; which will render a further provision necessary. The actual liberation of all our Citizens who were prisoners in Algiers, while it gratifies every feeling heart, is itself an earnest of a satisfactory termination of the whole negotiation. Measures are in operation for effecting Treaties with the Regencies of Tunis and Tripoli.

To an active external Commerce, the protection of a Naval force is indispensable. This is manifest with regard to Wars in which a State itself is a party. But besides this, it is in our own experience, that the most sincere Neutrality is not a sufficient guard against the depredations of Nations at War. To secure respect to a Neutral Flag, requires a Naval force, organized, and ready to vindicate it, from insult or aggression. This may even prevent the necessity of going to War, by discouraging belligerent Powers from committing such violations of the rights of the Neutral party, as may first or last, leave no other option. From the best information I have been able to obtain, it would seem as if our trade to the mediterranean, without a protecting force, will always be insecure; and our Citizens exposed to the calamities from which numbers of them have but just been relieved.

These considerations invite the United States, to look to the means, and to set about the gradual creation of a Navy. The increasing progress of their Navigation, promises them, at no distant period, the requisite supply of Seamen; and their means, in other respects, favour the undertaking. It is in encouragement, likewise, that their particular situation, will give weight and influence to a moderate Naval force in their hands. Will it not then be adviseable, to begin without delay, to provide, and lay up the materials for the building and equipping of Ships of War; and to proceed in the Work by degrees, in proportion as our resources shall render it practicable without inconvenience; so that a future War of Europe, may not find our Commerce in the same unprotected state, in which it was found by the present.

Congress have repeatedly, and not without success, directed their attention to the encouragement of Manufactures. The object is of too much consequence, not to insure a continuance of their efforts, in every way which shall appear eligible. As a general rule, Manufactures on public account, are inexpedient. But where the state of things in a Country, leaves little hope that certain branches of Manufacture will, for a great length of time obtain; when these are of a nature essential to the furnishing and equipping of the public force in time of War, are not establishments for procuring them on public account, *to the extent of the ordinary demand for the public service*, recommended by strong considerations of National policy, as an exception to the general rule? Ought our Country to remain in such cases, dependant on foreign supply, precarious, because liable to be interrupted? If the necessary Articles should, in this mode cost more in time of peace, will not the security and independence thence arising, form an ample compensation? Establishments of this sort, commensurate only with the calls of the public service in time of peace, will, in time of War, easily be extended in proportion to the exigencies of the Government; and may even perhaps be made to yield a surplus for the supply of our Citizens at large; so as to mitigate the privations from the interruption of their trade. If adopted, the plan ought to exclude all those branches which are already, or likely soon to be, established in the Country; in order that there may be no danger of interference with pursuits of individual industry.

It will not be doubted, that with reference either to individual, or National Welfare, Agriculture is of primary importance. In proportion as Nations advance in population, and other circum-stances of maturity, this truth becomes more apparent; and ren-ders the cultivation of the Soil more and more, an object of pub-lic patronage. Institutions for promoting it, grow up, supported by the public purse: and to what object can it be dedicated with greater propriety? Among the means which have been employed to this end, none have been attended with greater success than the establishment of Boards, composed of proper characters, charged with collecting and diffusing information, and enabled by premiums, and small pecuniary aids, to encourage and assist a spirit of discovery and improvement. This species of establish-ment contributes doubly to the increase of improvement; by stimulating to enterprise and experiment, and by drawing to a common centre, the results everywhere of individual skill and observation; and spreading them thence over the whole Nation. Experience accordingly has shewn, that they are very cheap In-struments, of immense National benefits.

I have heretofore proposed to the consideration of Congress, the expediency of establishing a National University, and also a Military Academy. The desirableness of both these Institutions, has so constantly increased with every new view I have taken of the subject, that I cannot omit the opportunity of once for all re-calling your attention to them.

The Assembly to which I address myself, is too enlightened not to be fully sensible how much a flourishing state of the Arts and Sciences, contributes to National prosperity and reputation. True it is, that our Country, much to its honor, contains many Seminaries of learning highly respectable and useful; but the funds upon which they rest, are too narrow, to command the ablest Professors, in the different departments of liberal knowl-edge, for the Institution contemplated, though they would be ex-cellent auxiliaries.

Amongst the motives to such an Institution, the assimilation of the principles, opinions and manners of our Countrymen, but the common education of a portion of our Youth from every quarter, well deserves attention. The more homogeneous our Citizens can be made in these particulars, the greater will be our prospect of permanent Union; and primary object of such a National Institution should be, the education of our Youth in the science of *Government*. In a Republic, what species of knowledge can be equally important? And what duty, more pressing on its Legislature, than to patronize a plan for communicating it to those, who are to be the future guardians of the liberties of the Country?

The Institution of a Military Academy, is also recommended by cogent reasons. However pacific the general policy of a Nation may be, it ought never to be without an adequate stock of Military knowledge for emergencies. The first would impair the energy of its character, and both would hazard its safety, or expose it to greater evils when War could not be avoided. Besides that War, might often, not depend upon its own choice. In proportion, as the observance of pacific maxims, might exempt a Nation from the necessity of practising the rules of the Military Art, ought to be its care in preserving, and transmitting by proper establishments, the knowledge of that Art. Whatever argument may be drawn from particular examples, superficially viewed, a thorough examination of the subject will evince, that the Art of War, is at once comprehensive and complicated; that it demands much previous study; and that the possession of it, in its most improved and perfect state, is always of great moment to the security of a Nation. This, therefore, ought to be a serious care of every Government: and for this purpose, an Academy, where a regular course of Instruction is given, is an obvious expedient, which different Nations have successfully employed.

The compensations to the Officers of the United States, in various instances, and in none more than in respect to the most important stations, appear to call for Legislative revision. The consequences of a defective provision, are of serious import to the Government. If private wealth, is to supply the defect of public retribution, it will greatly contract the sphere within which, the selection of Characters for Office, is to be made, and will proportionally diminish the probability of a choice of Men, able, as well as upright: Besides that it would be repugnant to the vital principles of our Government, virtually to exclude from public trusts, talents and virtue, unless accompanied by wealth.

While in our external relations, some serious inconveniences and embarrassments have been overcome, and others lessened, it is with much pain and deep regret I mention, that circumstances of a very unwelcome nature, have lately occurred. Our trade has suffered, and is suffering, extensive injuries in the West Indies, from the Cruisers, and Agents of the French Republic; and communications have been received from its Minister here, which indicate the danger of a further disturbance of our Commerce, by its authority; and which are, in other respects, far from agreeable.

It has been my constant, sincere, and earnest wish, in conformity with that of our Nation, to maintain cordial harmony, and a perfectly friendly understanding with that Republic. This wish remains unabated; and I shall persevere in the endeavour to fulfil it, to the utmost extent of what shall be consistent with a just, and indispensable regard to the rights and honour of our Country; nor will I easily cease to cherish the expectation, that a spirit of justice, candour and friendship, on the part of the Republic, will eventually ensure success.

In pursuing this course however, I cannot forget what is due to the character of our Government and Nation; or to a full and entire confidence in the good sense, patriotism, self-respect, and fortitude of my Countrymen.

I reserve for a special Message a more particular communication on this interesting subject.

Gentlemen of the House of Representatives: I have directed an estimate of the Appropriations, necessary for the service of the ensuing year, to be submitted from the proper Department; with a view of the public receipts and expenditures, to the latest period to which an account can be prepared.

It is with satisfaction I am able to inform you, that the Revenues of the United States continue in a state of progressive improvement.

A reinforcement of the existing provisions for discharging our public Debt, was mentioned in my Address at the opening of the last Session. Some preliminary steps were taken towards it, the maturing of which will, no doubt, engage your zealous attention during the present. I will only add, that it will afford me, heart felt satisfaction, to concur in such further measures, as will ascertain to our Country the prospect of a speedy extinguishment of the Debt. Posterity may have cause to regret, if, from any motive, intervals of tranquillity are left unimproved for accelerating this valuable end.

Gentlemen of the Senate, and of the House of Representatives: My solicitude to see the Militia of the United States placed on an efficient establishment, has been so often, and so ardently expressed, that I shall but barely recall the subject to your view on the present occasion; at the same time that I shall submit to your enquiry, whether our Harbours are yet sufficiently secured.

The situation in which I now stand, for the last time, in the midst of the Representatives of the People of the United States, naturally recalls the period when the Administration of the present form of Government commenced; and I cannot omit the occasion, to congratulate you and my Country, on the success of the experiment; nor to repeat my fervent supplications to the Supreme Ruler of the Universe, and Sovereign Arbiter of Nations, that his Providential care may still be extended to the United States; that the virtue and happiness of the People, may be preserved; and that the Government, which they have instituted, for the protection of their liberties, may be perpetual.

Reprinted from GW: Writings, 35: 310–12.

Index

~

About the Author

Don Higginbotham is Dowd Professor of History at the University of North Carolina at Chapel Hill. He has served as president of the Southern Historical Association and of the Society for Historians of the Early Republic. This is his third book on George Washington.